MW01644623

FOOD FOR THE SOUL

Devotions using food & cooking to illustrate Biblical truth

By annie keys

The Anointed Cook

Even the simplest meal can be an act of ministry. As you cook the food and prepare the plates, ask God to lead, bless and empower all who eat.

(James 5:16b --The prayer of a righteous person is powerful and effective.)

 This book can be purchased on Amazon.com

This book is also available as a devotional cookbook. These devotions PLUS favorite family recipes and cooking tips

Look for

FOOD FOR BODY AND SOUL

DEDICATION

To everybody who loves the Lord and enjoys food and cooking.

Credits

All material, words and photography, are the property of annie keys and the web site, Where the Rubber Meets the Road, by either authorship or permissions and may only be copied or printed in parts or pieces, not whole book and **may only be copied with book and author credit clearly stated.**

"Food for the Soul." may also be available in Afrikaans, translated with my permission by Casiveo/Pieter Jordaan.

Thank you to my Proof readers, you make me look good!: (in alphabetical order by first names)

"Barbara," Benjamin Lloyd, Carrie Messer, Dawna Moore, Deborah Swaringen, Fay Moore, Guyla Armstrong, Helen Curtis, and John Klyn,

Cover Photo: award winning photographer, Dawana Moore

Cover Design by: **Pieter Jordaan**

Cover Edit by: Dan Keys

Food for Thought

Inside each of us rages a battle between two strong beasts. One beast is driven by anger, bitterness, greed and rebellion.

The other beast is driven by love, generosity, responsibility, compassion and integrity.

Which beast will win the battle?

The one you feed.

(Native American Proverb)

Table of Contents

Psalms 34:8

Taste and see that the LORD is good, blessed is the one who takes refuge in him.

Good Lasagna Is Like Serving God

I John 5:3-5

One summer, my mother and I signed up for a low fat cooking class. The dish we were to prepare was low fat lasagna with whole wheat pasta. We were told that lasagna's main downfall was the obscene amount of fat contained in the dish.

Chef tapped her wooden spoon on the countertop and informed us that making a few low fat ingredient substitutions would not change the flavor. But, it would make the dish contain less than a third of the fat and half the calories. She assured us that the "lighter dish" would look and taste the same.

The instructor was right in that the lasagna looked the same as the real thing, at least at first glance. However, after several mouthfuls, the "lack" started to be noticed. The richness was missing and the "satisfied" feeling just never developed. It was mildly satisfying, but not as good as the original version.

Sometimes, we can think there are shortcuts and substitutions that can be made in serving God. When we search the scriptures to find "loop holes" so we can make substitutions; we deny the authority of God's Word.

When we look for easy Christianity, we are looking for permission to live the way we want to while expecting God's blessings to continue. The world lives by a different standard; God's laws are not hard laws. They are made for our good, to maintain healthy attitudes, relationships and activities.

I'm not talking about the "manmade" holiness that is dictated by hard rules. I'm talking about a committed Christ life, based on Biblical truth, not traditions and rules set by men. (Colossians 2:16-23)

God gives His Holy Spirit to convict of righteousness (John 16:8-10) and His Word to give us direction (2 Timothy 3:16-17). The body of Christ gives strength in fellowship (Hebrews 10:24-25) and through sound preaching and teaching; God works to confirm His Word (Mark 16:20).

God has provided all the resources that I need to live a committed Christ life and have an intimate relationship with Jesus. What I do with those resources is up to me; how I serve God is a personal decision. I will be held accountable for my own decisions and my own life choices.

I John 5:3-5

This is love for God: to obey his commands. And his commands are not burdensome, for everyone born of God overcomes the world. This is the victory that has overcome the world, even our faith. Who is it that overcomes the world? Only he who believes that Jesus is the Son of God.

Prayer:

Father, help me to live by the standards in your Word and not the standard of the world. Help me to recognize the difference between the traditions of man and the solid truth of scripture. Give me grace, purity and wisdom as I live each day for you. I love you. Amen.

Scriptural References:

Colossians 2:16-23

Therefore do not let anyone judge you by what you eat or drink, or with regard to a religious festival, a New Moon celebration or a Sabbath day. These are a shadow of the things that were to come; the reality, however, is found in Christ. Do not let anyone who delights in false humility and the worship of angels disqualify you. Such a person also goes into great detail about what they have seen; they are puffed up with idle notions by their unspiritual mind. They have lost connection with the head, from whom the whole body, supported and held together by its ligaments and sinews, grows as God causes it to grow.

Since you died with Christ to the elemental spiritual forces of this world, why, as though you still belonged to the world, do you submit to its rules: "Do not handle! Do not taste! Do not touch!"? These rules, which have to do with things that are all destined to perish with use, are based on merely human commands and teachings. Such regulations indeed have an appearance of wisdom, with their self-imposed worship, their false humility and their harsh treatment of the body, but they lack any value in restraining sensual indulgence.

John 16:8-10

When he comes, he will prove the world to be in the wrong about sin and righteousness and judgment: about sin, because people do not believe in me; about righteousness, because I am going to the Father, where you can see me no longer;

2 Timothy 3:16-17

All Scripture is God-breathed and is useful for teaching, rebuking, correcting and training in righteousness, so that the servant of God may be thoroughly equipped for every good work.

Hebrews 10:24-25

And let us consider how we may spur one another on toward love and good deeds, not giving up meeting together, as some are in the habit of doing, but encouraging one another—and all the more as you see the Day approaching.

Mark 16:20 Then the disciples went out and preached everywhere, and the Lord worked with them and confirmed his word by the signs that accompanied it.

Saints Are Like Good Chocolates

Mathew 25:28-30

They say that there are two kinds of people; those who love chocolate and those who just haven't tasted really good chocolate-- yet. When hovering over a box of fine chocolates, the only thought is the delight of the moment. However, a box of gourmet chocolates does not just magically appear all yummy and ready to be enjoyed.

The cocoa bean is huge and lumpy and almost impossible to crack open. Once the shell is open, there's no chocolate, as we know it, inside. The beans inside are hard, bitter and difficult to dig out. The delicious chocolates that look so perfect are a result of an intricate process.

Christian's are like cacao beans. We all start out "lumpy and raw." Like the box of wonderful chocolates, the Christians that we see as being so perfect have been through quite a bit of processing.

The learned saint who speaks with such passion and knowledge of God's Word was once fumbling through their Bible trying to find the book of Amos. Not even the Rev. Billy Graham sprang into ministry learned, experienced and accomplished.

Satan loves to hold a magnifying glass up to these saints. He also loves to whisper in my ear about how inept, useless and failing my own efforts are compared to "them." But, I must remember; even the most eloquent scholar was once a mumbling student.

To start with, God gives each of us talents according to the work He has called us to do (Matthew 25:15). Neither you nor I will ever be held up to another saint and compared to them. The most accomplished saint will be judged on the work they were given to do just as you and I will be judged on the work WE were given to do.

God will never compare my works to the works of others. What I accomplish will only be measured by the talent and directions I was, myself, given. In the parable of the talents, the master did not measure the servant with the least return by the servant with the most return. The master held each servant responsible for what they did with the talents they were, themselves, given (Matthew 25:19-23).

The only servant that was severely reprimanded was the one who did nothing at all with their own talents (Matthew 25:24-27). When satan convinces me to *not do anything* because I think that I can't do it right----or I can't do it as well as somebody else; the work that I was intended to do doesn't get done at all. And for THAT, I will be held accountable.

Mathew 25:28-30

Take the talent from him and give it to the one who has the ten talents. For everyone who has will be given more, and he will have an abundance. Whoever does not have, even what he has will be taken from him. And throw that worthless servant outside, into the darkness, where there will be weeping and gnashing of teeth.

Prayer:

Father, thank you that I won't be judged according to what others have accomplished. Help me to see the talents that you have given me. Show me how to use my talents to glorify you and serve you. I love you. Amen.

Scriptural References:

Matthew 25:15

To one he gave five bags of gold, to another two bags, and to another one bag, each according to his ability.

Matthew 25:19-23

After a long time the master of those servants returned and settled accounts with them. The man who had received five bags of gold brought the other five. 'Master,' he said, 'you entrusted me with five bags of gold. See, I have gained five more.'

"His master replied, 'Well done, good and faithful servant! You have been faithful with a few things; I will put you in charge of many things. Come and share your master's happiness!'

"The man with two bags of gold also came. 'Master,' he said, 'you entrusted me with two bags of gold; see, I have gained two more.'

"His master replied, 'Well done, good and faithful servant! You have been faithful with a few things; I will put you in charge of many things. Come and share your master's happiness!'

Matthew 25: 24-27

Then the man who had received one bag of gold came. 'Master,' he said, 'I knew that you are a hard man, harvesting where you have not sown and gathering where you have not scattered seed. So I was afraid and went out and hid your gold in the ground. See, here is what belongs to you.'

"His master replied, 'You wicked, lazy servant! So you knew that I harvest where I have not sown and gather where I have not scattered seed? Well then, you should have put my money on deposit with the bankers, so that when I returned I would have received it back with interest.

Don't be Lunch Meat

I Peter 5:8-9

While at the zoo with my grandson, Quinlan, he told me all about lions. The lion only gets involved in the hunt when the prey is too large for the lionesses to bring down.

Those who hunt lions say that a lion roars from a distance, arrogantly letting his prey know that he's on the hunt— and you're on the menu. The apostle, Peter, compared satan to a roaring lion looking to see who he can devour.

Like the stalking lion, satan thinks he has us cornered. Satan can NOT *make* us sin. But, he does know our weaknesses and he hopes that we don't know how to defend ourselves. The scripture says to be self-controlled and alert; *we are led aside and tempted* ***by our own flesh***. (James 1: 12-15)

When we hold all of our attitudes and actions up before the revealing light of God's Word, we are far less likely to fall to temptation. "No temptation has overtaken you except such as is common to man; but God is faithful, who will not allow you to be tempted beyond what you are able, but with the temptation will also make the way of escape, that you may be able to bear it." (I Corinthians 10:13)

Satan has no power over us that we don't allow him to take. Sin has no levels, all sin, whether little or big, separates us from God's presence. When we are faithful to read God's Word, we know satan's tricks. (II Corinthians 2:10-11) No matter how fiercely satan roars: his ability to devour us is determined by our willingness to cooperate with his temptations! Refuse to be lunch meat for the devil.

I Peter 5:8-9

Be self-controlled and alert. Your enemy, the devil, prowls around like a roaring lion looking for someone to devour. Resist him, standing firm in the faith, because you know that your brothers throughout the world are undergoing the same kind of sufferings.

Prayer:

Father, I love you and I'm so thankful that you love me. Help me to always recognize the devil's traps and to follow your instructions. Amen.

James 1:12-15

Blessed is the one who perseveres under trial because, having stood the test, that person will receive the crown of life that the Lord has promised to those who love him.

When tempted, no one should say, "God is tempting me." For God cannot be tempted by evil, nor does he tempt anyone; but each person is tempted when they are dragged away by their own evil desire and enticed. [15] Then, after desire has conceived, it gives birth to sin; and sin, when it is full-grown, gives birth to death.

I Corinthians 10:13

No temptation has overtaken you except what is common to mankind. And God is faithful; he will not let you be tempted beyond what you can bear. But when you are tempted, he will also provide a way out so that you can endure it.

II Corinthians 2:10-11

Anyone you forgive, I also forgive. And what I have forgiven—if there was anything to forgive—I have forgiven in the sight of Christ for your sake, in order that Satan might not outwit us. For we are not unaware of his schemes.

("Don't Be Lunch Meat" is also in, "Life Is Like Buffalo Breath," A devotional with stories about animals to show Biblical truth. Includes photography illustrations. (available from Amazon.)

Hot Lemon Prayer

Hebrews 4:9-11

Did you know that a lemon explodes when it gets hot? Neither did I, until today. Since I'd forgotten to put the lemons for a pie out to warm to room temperature, I decided to put the fruit in the microwave. If the lemon is at room temp, the juice is released more readily.

In my haste to get the pie started, I must have set the microwave on three minutes instead of three seconds—and walked away. The lemons exploded like citrus hand grenades; blowing the door on the appliance open and spraying hot lemon juice all over my kitchen! Instead of hastening the pie prep, I'd prolonged it. What an AWFUL mess.

Sometimes, I have the same attitude about answers to prayer as I had about the pie, fast is better. God has all the time in eternity. He doesn't have a list on his fridge headed, "Things I MUST do today." God is much more concerned about our relationship with Him than He is with our immediate pleasure and comfort.

Sometimes, when we pray, we demand things to start (or stop) RIGHT NOW! We fail to understand that when we let God be in control of our lives, everything happens under His loving supervision. (Proverbs 3:5-6) Both the good and the bad in our lives work for the long term goal of making us into the image of Christ.

When we take matters into our own hands and start trying to "be God" instead of wait for God, like the lemons in the microwave, we can make a mess. In Hebrews, God's Word says that we know we have entered into His rest *when we have ceased from our labors.*

This does not mean that we put aside ministry and just sit down. Nor does it mean we turn a blind eyeball toward sin. It means that we give our problems, plans and ambitions to God and wait for His direction while doing the things that are "my part;" like preparing, planning and when in the case of sin, prayerful intervention.

God doesn't forget us, sometimes, it takes time to get us ready and time for the circumstances to be just right for God's plan to unfold. When we enter into God's rest, we trust that He knows what He is doing and simply follow His directions; even when it takes longer than what we thought it would. (Isaiah 40:31)

Hebrews 4:9-11

There remains, then, a Sabbath-rest for the people of God; for anyone who enters God's rest also rests from his own work, just as God did from his. Let us, therefore, make every effort to enter that rest, so that no one will fall by following their example of disobedience.

Prayer: Father God, help me to be patient with myself and with your plan for my life. Encourage me through Bible study and fellowship. Confirm in my heart that your ways are not my ways but your ways always work out for the best in my life. I want your perfect will for my life. Amen.

Scriptural References:

Proverbs 3:5-6

Trust in the Lord with all your heart, and do not lean on your own understanding. In all your ways acknowledge him, and he will make your path straight.

Isaiah 40:31

They that wait upon the Lord shall renew their strength. They shall mount up with wings as an eagle. They shall run and not be weary, they shall walk and not faint.

Making Yummy from Crummy

Genesis 50:20

My daughter and I were baking a cake to take to a church fellowship dinner. We'd baked a sheet cake and decided to turn it out onto a flat board and ice it prettily. To our horror, when I went to dump the cake from the pan, it fell out in pieces!

Not just a few pieces that could have been held together with a spoonful of icing and no harm done. The cake lay across the counter top like a firecracker had gone off in the pan. In despair, we scooped the crumbles into a big bowl and set it aside. There was no time to bake another cake, we had no choice but to stop and buy a store bought cake on the way to church.

Disappointed, but in agreement as to our only option, my daughter reached into the bowl of crumbs and popped an experimental handful into her mouth. She said, "Wow, mama, it's too bad it fell a part because that is really *good* cake."

Tasting the cake myself, I agreed. With sudden inspiration, I grabbed a decorative glass bowl out of the cabinet. Opening the pantry door, I told my daughter that the only problem the cake had was that it had been torn up.

Selecting a can of cherry pie filling and a box of vanilla pudding from the panty, I then took a carton of whipping cream from the fridge. We began a bona fide food experiment; also known as, dessert damage control.

We whipped the cream, made the pudding and opened the can of cherry filling. Layering the ingredients in the glass bowl we created an elegant looking dessert that was absolutely delicious. If we hadn't known the mess we started with, we'd have had no clue this tasty and lovely dessert was ever anything but, well, tasty and lovely. What had started as an intervention experiment had turned out to be a fabulous dessert.

God does the same thing for me when my life gets messed up. Stuff happens. Sometimes I cause my own "mess," sometimes circumstances I have no control over tears my life up. Other times, I get hurt simply because somebody else pulled me into "their" mess. Regardless of how I get broken, it hurts. Experience has taught me that if I don't deal with the mess, I can become depressed, angry and even bitter.

God's plan for my life is success. Throughout History, God has taken broken lives and made them into beautiful testimonies. No matter how bad the mess is; if I let him, God will make it work for His good and mine (Romans 8:28). Satan's plan for my life is destruction and pain. When I give my life to Jesus, no matter what the circumstances, in time, God will show me good in it. (Jeremiah 29:11)

The next time you find yourself in a crummy mess, instead of being angry, engage in an experiment. Take a deep breath, step back, hand the broken crumbs of your life to God and say, "You, my Lord, can fix this, show me what you want me to do." It will be an experiment that can't fail, I promise.

Genesis 50:20

You intended to harm me, but God intended it for good to accomplish what is now being done, the saving of many lives.

Prayer:

Father, open my eyes so that I can see that there is no thing in life that is beyond your care. You will take whatever hurtful circumstances that surround me and use them to mold me in to the vessel you want me to be. Thank you for loving me and making bad things work out for my good. Amen.

Scriptural references:

Romans 8:28

And we know that in all things God works for the good of those who love him, who have been called according to his purpose.

Jeremiah 29:

For I know the plans I have for you," declares the LORD, "plans to prosper you and not to harm you, plans to give you hope and a future.

Making Healthy Choices

II Peter 1: 4-9

I love going to the big warehouse stores like Sam's Club and Costco. My favorite time to go is on the days when they have vendors set up with little cooking stations.

One reason this is a favorite time to shop is because they have new and creative ways to prepare old favorites alongside samples of food I've never eaten.

As I pass by, the vendors offer me tasty morsels to sample. I love learning new methods and experiencing new tastes. However, there is also a "down side" to shopping on this "sample it" day.

The whole idea of this presentation is once I have a taste, I discover that it's so good I want to have more. Since I shop here often, I'm aware of the temptations and make sure I'm satisfied with healthy food *before* I get there so that the samples are eaten sparingly.

Food is one of my weaknesses, I dearly love yummy food. An important part of being a mature adult is that I have the wisdom to know I should turn and walk away when I'm tempted. When I discipline myself to make healthy life style choices, I reap the physical benefits.

Now and then, I blow my plan totally, but I know how important it is to pick up and keep on going. Stumbling is not failure; the only time I fail is when I don't get back up and continue on.

The Bible says that the fruit of the Spirit is SELF control. (Galatians 5:22-23) And Proverbs 24:16 says though I stumble, I will get up. Even though the verse refers to spiritual stumbles, I reference it for my physical fallings as well. God cares about EVERY area of my life.

In the same manner, when I discipline myself to make healthy spiritual choices, I reap the benefits of being spiritually stronger, healthier and more alert. I need to plan for Bible study and prayer the same way I plan how I will turn aside and walk away from temptation.

Life is about discipline, anything worthwhile requires discipline and planning to make it a routine part of my life. Just like physical exercise makes my body muscles strong, Bible study and conversation with my Lord exercises my faith and makes my spiritual muscles strong. (Romans 10:17)

The discipline of choosing healthy food choices makes a healthy body. The discipline of spiritual choices makes a strong, effective witness and a successful life. Make a plan, stick to the plan, reap the benefits; it's ALL good, "gotta get me some more of THAT!"

II Peter 1: 4-9

Through these he has given us his very great and precious promises, so that through them you may participate in the divine nature and escape the corruption in the world caused by evil desires.

For this very reason, make every effort to add to your faith goodness; and to goodness, knowledge; and to knowledge, self-control; and to self-control, perseverance; and to perseverance, godliness; and to godliness, brotherly kindness; and to brotherly kindness, love.

For if you possess these qualities in increasing measure, they will keep you from being ineffective and unproductive in your knowledge of our Lord Jesus Christ. But if anyone does not have them, he is nearsighted and blind, and has forgotten that he has been cleansed from his past sins.

Prayer:

Lord Jesus, help me to discipline my life so that I make healthy choices both spiritually and physically. Open my eyes so I'm aware of temptation and can respond quickly with the fruit of the Spirit, self control. Help me to be strong and healthy in every area of my life. I love you. Amen

Scriptural References:

Galatians 5:22-23

But the fruit of the Spirit is love, joy, peace, forbearance, kindness, goodness, faithfulness, gentleness and self-control. Against such things there is no law.

Proverbs 24:16

Though a righteous man falls seven times, he will get up, but the wicked will stumble into ruin.

Romans 10:17

Consequently, faith comes from hearing the message, and the message is heard through the word about Christ.

Things Go Better With Jesus

II Corinthians 4:7

My friend and I were on a tour of the Coca Cola bottling plant. The final feature of the tour was the product museum. Every flavor of coke ever created was featured for a "tasting."

We were enjoying our tasting tour, moving down the line cafeteria style. It was surprising to see how many flavors had been made compared to the number of flavors that actually made it into production.

Lively music was playing and my friend and I were dancing along, tasting and giggling. Her comments on some of the crazy flavors that "never passed the taste test" were making me laugh. We were giggling like a couple of school girls.

Turning forward to make sure there were no obstacles to trip over, I found myself nose to nose with the woman in front of me. As I made an ecstatic utterance of surprise the lady also squealed and then, SLAM, I ran slap into -------the mirror.

There had been no lady in front of me; it had been my own reflection! When I hit the mirrored glass wall, I lost my balance, fell backwards on my rear and threw the beverage all over my own face. For a moment I had no idea what had happened.

Needless to say, everybody, including me, laughed at the crazy woman sprawled on the floor with Coke dripping from her nose. The mirror had not only been the cause of my misfortune, it served to display my undignified landing to everybody in the room. Mercy; I was a SIGHT, laying there blinking my eyeballs.

Life has its share of embarrassing moments. Many of our moments of humiliation come because we don't recognize our own reflection. Involved in our own life, we are unaware of how what we are doing looks to those around us. Sometimes God puts a "mirror" in front of us so that we have no choice but look at ourselves. The reality check can sometimes be pretty surprising.

Satan loves to take these moments that are so much a necessary part of life and magnify them, point to them and use them to tear down our confidence and humiliate us. One of satan's favorite taunts is, "you look stupid!" Genesis 1:27 says we are created in God's image; notice the basis of the insult?

What better time to realize that 'stuff' happens to us all! No person alive ever lived without an embarrassing moment at some point in their life; more often than not—there are MANY.

When God reveals how I look to others and to Him, I sometimes need to work on the image I am reflecting. When I look through the Biblical perspective of self esteem I see myself realistically and accept myself as I am; fragile in my humanity while perfect in Christ. No need for self-condemnation but much need for living my commitment to the Christ life. The world focuses on outward appearances, the scripture focuses on how God sees me--- perfect through the blood of Jesus.

II Corinthians 4:7

But we have this treasure in jars of clay to show that this all-surpassing power is from God and not from us.

Prayer:

Father God, forgive me for the times that I've ignored the example you set and followed my own will. Help me to understand that to look like and act like the world is not the way you created me. I'm to represent you in all that I do. Thank you for the convicting voice of your Holy Spirit. Amen.

Scriptural References:

<u>Genesis 1:27</u>

So God created mankind in his own image, in the image of God he created them; male and female he created them.

God's Mysterious Ways

Romans 8:38-39

A friend gave me the happy news that one of her co-workers had started coming to my church. She told me the woman's name, described her and asked me if I would look for her to personally welcome her.

The next weekend, I baked a loaf of bread as a friendship gift and after church; I looked for "Debbie." Matching the friend's description to a new face at church, I went to the young woman and said, "Debbie?"

She looked surprised saying that, yes, she was Debbie. I hugged her and said I was SO happy to meet her and that I'd baked a loaf of bread for her. "Debbie" started crying and telling me that I had no idea how much that meant to her.

As it turned out, she was not my friend's co-worker, "Debbie." The lady I gave the bread to was a visitor that had been through a lot of trials and hard times. It seemed that everything she had done had resulted in failure and she was emotionally broken. She was wondering if God really knew her situation and even was questioning in her heart if God actually loved her at all.

When a total stranger at a church she had never gone to before, called her BY NAME and gifted her a loaf of bread, she knew that only God could have arranged such a meeting. As it worked out, both of the new "Debbies" at church became a friend to me. God is good.

God cares about every part of life that we walk through and is sovereign over all. He who calls the stars by name (Ps. 147:4 & Isaiah 40:26) and knows when a sparrow falls from its nest (Matt. 10:29), also knows the number of hairs on my head (Luke 12:7)

Even the things that satan plans to ruin my relationship with God and wreck my life, <u>can</u> be worked for good (Genesis 50:20). Romans 8:28 says, "And we know that in all things God works for the good of those who love him, who have been called according to his purpose."

When I trust in the sovereignty of my Lord, nothing that happens in my life is useless or wasted! His ability to take every situation, every circumstance and use it for my <u>good</u> is my assurance that I can live victoriously. It is only <u>my choice</u> that can <u>allow</u>

satan's temporary plan for destruction to separate me from God's loving plan for my life.

Romans 8:38-39

For I am convinced that neither death nor life, neither angels nor demons, neither the present nor the future, nor any powers, neither height nor depth, nor anything else in all creation, will be able to separate us from the love of God that is in Christ Jesus our Lord.

Prayer:

Father God, your ways are far too great for me to understand. Help me to be sensitive to your Spirit so you can use me to encourage others. Thank you for caring so much about our lives. I love you. Amen

Scriptural References:

Psalms 147:4

He determines the number of the stars and calls them each by name.

Isaiah 40:26

Lift up your eyes and look to the heavens: Who created all these? He who brings out the starry host one by one and calls forth each of them by name. Because of his great power and mighty strength, not one of them is missing.

Matt. 10:29

Are not two sparrows sold for a penny? Yet not one of them will fall to the ground outside your Father's care.

Luke 12:7

Indeed, the very hairs of your head are all numbered. Don't be afraid; you are worth more than many sparrows.

Genesis 50:20

You intended to harm me, but God intended it for good to accomplish what is now being done, the saving of many lives.

The Forgotten Shrimp

Matthew 5:23-24

One afternoon, I went to get shrimp from the freezer to prepare for dinner that night. Even though I was sure I'd bought a bag of shrimp, I found no shrimp in the freezer. Thinking perhaps I'd not bought the shrimp after all; I fixed something else for our meal.

Days later, I was horrified to find the package of thawed; now bubbling with bacteria---shrimp in the bottom of a bag, beside the washer in the laundry room! EWWW! Now, I know what happened to the shrimp.

The day I'd bought the seafood, I'd taken advantage of a great sale on fluffy bath towels. Once home, I put the sack of towels beside the laundry basket to wash before use. It never crossed my mind that the sales clerk would put a bag of frozen shrimp in with a pile of bath towels.

I wonder how long it would have been before the 'gases' from the shrimp built up in that sealed bag and it exploded. Can you IMAGINE what that would be like? **BANG!** Smelly rotting shrimp spewing everywhere; nasty!

Sometimes, we stuff hurtful things that people have said or done to us down inside our heart, out of sight. Instead of taking our pain to Jesus for resolution, we hide it. We make a point to not think about the pain and anger or the broken relationship; keeping ourselves busy so we don't remember.

Scripture shows that our relationships with each other do affect our relationship with God; whether the rift exists because of our <u>own</u> apathy or the carelessness of somebody else. Mark 12:28-31 says the two most important life laws are, love God <u>and</u> love each other. The Bible also reveals that anger with your spouse can hinder your prayers. (I Peter 3:7)

If left unattended to, stuffed in the bottom of our heart, unresolved anger will eventually explode; spewing ugly bitter words and hurt feelings everywhere. Stuffing anger and hurt feelings inside our heart and ignoring them never ends well.

The only cure for wounded relationships is to turn them over to the Holy Spirit for handling. The Spirit knows God's perfect will and can direct our heart on how to heal and rebuild broken relationships.

Satan loves it when we have bitterness and anger hiding in the bottom of our heart. Deal with the hurt feelings now, before they explode and make a big mess; take them to Jesus.

Matthew 5:23-24

If therefore you are presenting your offering at the altar, and there remember that your brother has something against you, leave your offering there before the altar, and go your way; first be reconciled to your brother, and then come and present your offering.

Prayer:

Father God, help me to realize that anytime I have a "people" problem, I compromise my relationship with you. Show me how to keep my friendships clear of conflict and help me to forgive others when they have done me wrong. Remind me that there is no issue too big OR too small to lay at the foot of the cross. Amen.

Scripture References

Mark 12:28-31

One of the teachers of religious law was standing there listening to the debate. He realized that Jesus had answered well, so he asked, "Of all the commandments, which is the most important?"

Jesus replied, "The most important commandment is this: 'Listen, O Israel! The LORD our God is the one and only LORD. And you must love the LORD your God with all your heart, all your soul, all your mind, and all your strength.' The second is equally important: 'Love your neighbor as yourself.' No other commandment is greater than these."

I Peter 3:7

Husbands, in the same way be considerate as you live with your wives, and treat them with respect as the weaker partner and as heirs with you of the gracious gift of life, so that nothing will hinder your prayers.

Mmmmmm Pie!

Psalm 32:5

My grandson was reading his library book. He read, "Mrs. Hen put the apple pie, mmmmmmm, on the table to cool." The sentence actually was, "Mrs. Hen put the apple pie on the table to cool." There was no guttural utterance, mmmmm, indicated. I stopped him and asked him to read the sentence again.

Once more, he added the "mmmm" after apple pie. I told him to look carefully; there was no "mmmm" in the story. He explained to me that he knew that, but he just couldn't help it! When his mouth said "apple pie," his mind made him say, "mmmmmm" because he ate some apple pie once and he loves it so much.

Like the apple pie, Gods presence, His provision and direction, should be reflected on. In scripture, the word, Selah, is found in the Psalms 71 times and in Habakkuk three times. Selah is thought to mean: "think about this" or "pause and reflect." God lives in our praises. This does not mean that He has a house with glory paneling and “bless you Lord!” paint. To ‘live in’ means to have substance, to come alive in.

When my grandson thought of apple pie, his memory put substance to the thought. He could remember the fragrance; perhaps even taste the cinnamon and cloves dancing on the back of his tongue. When we praise God, our memory rushes to the forefront, reminding us of the times that God has delivered, instructed and directed.

As David wrote the Psalms, out of his own past experience, he remembered God’s power. Because he had a relationship with God, he could recall the Lord’s majesty and power when he was frightened or lonely. The memory made God’s presence come alive again, right then, “now,” and he was encouraged and comforted.

Selah is also a music term that means, “to pause or reflect.” It can mean an instrumental prelude, you know, ‘background music’ while you think about it. The next time you see the term, “Selah,” reread the verse, think about how God’s servant, David, had stopped to think about what you just read. Then, pause and remember the last time God delivered, protected or glorified His presence in your own life and praise Him. God inhabits (comes alive, has substance in) our praise.

Psalm 32:5

“Then I acknowledged my sin to you and did not cover up my iniquity. I said, "I will confess my transgressions to the LORD"-- and you forgave the guilt of my sin. Selah”

Prayer:

Father God, thank you for all of the times you have saved me from the traps of the enemy. Thank you for delivering me and giving me direction. The next time I stand in fear help me to think about all the times you have intervened in my life. Amen.

Step One: START

I Corinthians 9:27

Today, I made a decision. Not only am I going to watch what I eat, I'm also going to join an aerobic exercise group. Stopping by the gym to pick up the program syllabus, I was invited to observe an on-going class. As I stood, watching the tiny little instructor, I made two observations.

#1. Assuming that if I could even find that stretchy little aerobics outfit in my size, I'd look like 100 pounds of Jell-O struggling to get out of a 25 pound sack.

#2. It would take a crane to get me off the floor when I fell, and prancing around like that, falling is an absolute certainty.

Thoroughly frustrated yet painfully aware of the need to change my lifestyle; I remembered a conversation I'd had with an inmate at the county jail while I was doing the jail ministry. She'd recently accepted Christ and was struggling with many life style changes. She was overwhelmed with the things that would need to be different.

With the insight of the Holy Spirit, I told her that she should stop looking at ALL the stuff that she thought she had to change and begin to focus on ONE thing. Start. A good place to start is with the Word of God.

The Word of God changes your heart. Once the heart is changed, attitudes change. No matter how strong worldly habits or how deep the scars, faithful daily exposure to God's Word will, in time, heal, deliver and direct.

The important part is to plan a quiet time each day, pick up the Bible and---start. As scripture comes alive in the heart, attitudes begin to reflect the heart of God and change is natural.

Exercise and diet are the same way; at my age and weight, I can't suddenly start running marathons and eating only water and carrot sticks. I've set a time each day to walk; PLANNING is essential to success. IF I remain faithful to my commitment, my whole lifestyle WILL change. I just need to--- start.

I Corinthians 9:27

I don't know about you, but I'm running hard for the finish line. I'm giving it everything I've got. No sloppy living for me! I'm staying alert and in top condition. I'm not going to get caught napping, telling everyone else all about it and then missing out myself. (The Message)

Prayer:

My Lord, you are a holy God that cannot look upon sin. Help me to know that you don't expect me to change myself; you send me the Holy Spirit to tell me not only what to change, but how to make the changes. Give me ears to hear and a heart to listen so that I will yield myself to your directions. Thank you. I love you for loving me too much to leave me the way I am. Amen

Not Shopping HERE Anymore!

James 2:12-13

That's it; I'm going to shop someplace else. There is NO way that I'm ever going to go to that grocery store again. That woman that checked out her groceries beside me, she—she---she is a *hypocrite*! She claims to be a great cook and she just bought a box of INSTANT macn'cheese. Hmmfff,

Sounds crazy, doesn't it? Why is it that the only place being with hypocrites bothers us is <u>at church</u>? None of us are without sin. I John 1:8 says if we say we don't sin, we lie and Christ is not in us. <u>All</u> of us have the <u>potential</u> to be a hypocrite.

When I go to church, I fellowship with people who are just like "me," saved by God's mercy and grace. Jesus died so He could have a relationship with all of us. The Word says that God does not want <u>even ***one***</u> person to perish, God wants <u>*all*</u> people to come to know Jesus as their savior. (II Peter 3:9) No exceptions.

Christians are warned to examine our own hearts *before* we look for sin in others. (Matthew 7:3-5) However we are to discern what sin is and not ignore it.

The Word gives instructions on how to handle sin in our own life and direction for addressing sin within the body of Christ. (Luke 17: 3-4) There is no scripture that says that I should avoid going to church because there are sinners there.

Satan's job is to discourage us from fellowship with the body of Christ. His favorite tool is a magnifying glass. Satan makes sure that we see every tiny flaw in the people sitting on the pew beside us *and* in the pulpit before us. Satan knows how easily we humans are distracted and makes full use of that knowledge.

The devil is the accuser of the brethren (Revelation 12:10) and he delights to point out the personal preference issues we have with the music director, the pastor's hair and clothes, whether or not the flowers are real and even what color the carpet is. These things may irritate us simply because of our personal tastes or preference, *but to what point*?

There is no scripture declaring that Hell is filled with people who don't sing out of hymnals or don't put real flowers on the altar. There is no corner in Hell reserved for those pastors who dare to stand in the pulpit without a suit and tie.

When I can be so easily distracted about the things that really just do NOT matter—and ignore the fact that my neighbors are lost and going to Hell; satan is absolutely giddy with delight.

The Holy Spirit's job is to convict individuals of ***sin***, not instruct them about their wardrobe choices or their music style selections. Our job is to pray and, if possible, gently restore those who have fallen into sin; while being careful that we don't fall into temptation ourselves. (Galatians 6:1)

If I'm not diligent in searching my own heart and attitudes; I can find myself going to church as a Pharisee. Pharisees went to "church" to find evidence for use in proving others wrong instead of looking for truth that would teach them how to live right.

Pharisees were concerned about appearances. They had no care about loving God and no interest in serving with hearts of compassion. (Luke 18:9-12)

When I stand before the Lord on that great Day of Judgment, I will be asked what I did to build His church; to lead the lost—including the hypocrites—to Jesus.

He will want to know what I did to minister to the needs of the poor, the sick and the hurting. He will be looking at my faithfulness, my compassion and my desire to be a Christ like example to those around me.

Did I have mercy and work as a servant? Did I help leadership to fulfill the ministry of Christ? Or did I nitpick everything, whine about things that didn't matter and pout with self-righteousness?

God will never ever ask me to explain why there were hypocrites going to my church. He will ask why I never tried to love them to Jesus. And if I didn't, then won't it be I who was the hypocrite?

James 2:12-13

So speak and so act as those who are to be judged under the law of liberty. For judgment is without mercy to one who has shown no mercy. Mercy triumphs over judgment.

Prayer: Lord Jesus, show me my own heart so I can ask your forgiveness. Help me to show mercy to the lost, no matter where I find them. Help me to show the love of God through acts of compassion and encouragement. Thank you for your patience with me as I learn to let Christ minister through me..

Scriptural References:

I John 1:8

If we claim to be without sin, we deceive ourselves and the truth is not in us.

II Peter 3:9

The Lord is not slow in keeping his promise, as some understand slowness. Instead he is patient with you, not wanting anyone to perish, but everyone to come to repentance.

Matthew 7:3-5

Why do you look at the speck of sawdust in your brother's eye and pay no attention to the plank in your own eye? How can you say to your brother, 'Let me take the speck out of your eye,' when all the time there is a plank in your own eye? You hypocrite, first take the plank out of your own eye, and then you will see clearly to remove the speck from your brother's eye.

Luke 17:3-4

So watch yourselves. If your brother or sister sins against you, rebuke them; and if they repent, forgive them. Even if they sin against you seven times in a day and seven times come back to you saying 'I repent,' you must forgive them.

Revelation 12;10

Then I heard a loud voice in heaven say: "Now have come the salvation and the power and the kingdom of our God, and the authority of his Messiah. *For the accuser of our brothers and sisters, who accuses them before our God day and night*, has been hurled down.

Galatians 6:1

Brothers and sisters, if someone is caught in a sin, you who live by the Spirit should restore that person gently. But watch yourselves, or you also may be tempted.

Luke 18:9-12

To some who were confident of their own righteousness and looked down on everyone else, Jesus told this parable, "Two men went up to the temple to pray, one a Pharisee and the other a tax collector. The Pharisee stood by himself and prayed: 'God, I thank you that I am not like other people—robbers, evildoers, adulterers—or even like this tax collector. I fast twice a week and give a tenth of all I get.

Make a Pie Out of Those Lemons

Galatians 5: 22-23

Has anybody ever hurt your feelings or made you just down right MAD? Have you ever had your life messed up by circumstances that you have no control over? Do you ever feel like life is just—not---fair? Sometimes, stuff happens in life that can make your heart bitter as a lemon!

There is a saying that when life hands you lemons, make a pie. However, making a pie requires effort and determination. A mile high lemon meringue pie doesn't just miraculously appear because you acknowledge that you'd like to have one. Making a lemon pie takes effort, action, patience and work; but, it's ALWAYS worth it.

Satan wants the trials of life to make us bitter. Anger is one of satan's tools (Ephesians 4:26-27). Proverbs 29:11 says that *fools* look for revenge. Romans 12:19 specifically says to NOT get revenge; let God handle it. Psalms 4:4 says anger can lead to sin, it's best to be silent. All that makes sense, but, taking action and making a change is not so easy. God knows that.

When we are angry at people, that anger separates us from intimacy with Jesus. (Matthew 5: 23) Satan wants to use sour circumstances to drive a wedge between us and our Savior. We DO have the choice of what we do with the sour things in life. Satan can't ***make*** us do or feel anything; he can only *try* to influence our thoughts. My actions and attitudes can only be changed by---me.

I can allow bitterness to make my heart mean, hard, callous and vengeful. Or I can do the things necessary to change the bitterness into tenderness and sweetness. This is an actual physical, emotional and mental choice that only I can make for myself.

Action is required; bitterness will only destroy if left unattended to. I must first prayerfully plan then actually do the things that turn the bitter into better. It takes conscious effort but, with determination I can get busy and make something good out of those lemons. What ARE the things I must do to make this bitter event, this anger inside of me---into sweetness?

Prayer is the first step toward transforming bitter fruit into the fruit of the Spirit. I ask God to help me forgive the person I'm angry with. Remember, Ephesians 6:12 says that we don't fight against flesh and blood, but against the devil. When I forgive rather than get revenge, I am taking action to turn the bitter fruit of anger into the sweetness of the fruit of the Spirit.

One of the hardest parts of forgiveness is---"forgetness." When I truly forgive, I make a conscious effort to <u>not</u> revisit the circumstance that caused my pain. One of my favorite verses for "forgetness" is Philippians 3:13-14.

Sometimes, when the hurt is very bad, I have even physically taken my hand and turned my face away as a symbolic action. A physical reminder that *I no longer look at that event*. I look at Jesus who forgives and heals every wound, in full realization that I have to ***let*** *Him do those things*.

<u>Galatians 5: 22-23</u>

But the fruit of the Spirit is love, joy, peace, patience, kindness, goodness, faithfulness, gentleness and self-control. Against such things there is no law.

<u>Prayer:</u>

Lord Jesus, forgive me when I become angry and help me to know how to turn the bitter things in life into the sweet fruit of the Spirit. Show me how to forgive and to forget. Show me how to build instead of destroy. In Jesus' name. Amen.

Scriptural References:

Ephesians 4:26-27

In your anger do not sin. Do not let the sun go down while you are still angry, [and] do not give the devil a foothold

Proverbs 29:11

Fools give full vent to their rage but the wise bring calm in the end.

Romans 12:19

Do not take revenge, my dear friends, but leave room for God's wrath, for it is written: "It is mine to avenge; I will repay," says the Lord.

Psalms 4:4

Tremble and do not sin; when you are on your beds, search your hearts and be silent.

Matthew 5:23-24

Therefore, if you are offering your gift at the altar and there remember that your brother or sister has something against you, leave your gift there in front of the altar. First go and be reconciled to them; then come and offer your gift.

Ephesians 6:12

For our struggle is not against flesh and blood, but against the rulers, against the authorities, against the powers of this dark world and against the spiritual forces of evil in the heavenly realms.

Philippians 3:13-14 Brothers and sisters, I do not consider myself yet to have taken hold of it. But one thing I do: Forgetting what is behind and straining toward what is ahead, I press on toward the goal to win the prize for which God has called me heavenward in Christ Jesus.

Got To Be Less of Me

Galatians 5: 16-18

Since I struggle with my weight, I'm constantly searching for ways to make dieting easier. Experience has taught me that no matter how much I pay for diets and gym memberships, there is only one absolute method for success: the self-discipline to eat less, exercise more. It works every time.

One of the diet "clubs" that I've joined through the years was called, "Less of Me." The group provided the encouragement of fellowship with others who struggled just like I did. There is great strength in fellowship with people who know exactly what I'm going through.

John the Baptist spoke of Jesus saying, "He must increase and I must decrease" (John 3:30). The difference between the spiritual "less of me" concept and the weight loss version is; with Jesus, there's something to fill the void.

Jesus loved us so much that He gave His life that we could know HIM intimately. More than just the surface relationship of supportive friends at a weight loss group; an intimate emotional relationship like a husband loves his wife.

Like eating less and staying physically fit, spiritual fitness requires self-discipline. We should challenge ourselves; make a conscious effort to make "more of Jesus" one of our daily goals. Just like a plan for physical fitness, it will require both discipline and action.

As difficult as it is to set a time for daily exercise; setting a time for daily Bible study and prayer can be even more of a challenge. The first step is to make a plan; but the most important step is to DO it.

Nothing I do that benefits my physical self or my spiritual self is easy to accomplish. The old adage, "no pain no gain" holds true in many areas of life, including doing the things that make me both physically AND spiritually healthy.

However, the "less of me more of Jesus" concept has not only a benefit for today but for eternity as well. The inner self wants to be physically and spiritually healthy, but without hands on discipline, both will fail. More of Jesus, less of ---me; like a successful diet and exercise plan, requires not only motivation but also planning <u>and</u> participation.

Galatians 5: 16-18

So I say, live by the Spirit, and you will not gratify the desires of the sinful nature. For the sinful nature desires what is contrary to the Spirit, and the Spirit what is contrary to the sinful nature. They are in conflict with each other, so that you do not do what you want. But if you are led by the Spirit, you are not under law.

Prayer:

Lord Jesus, help me to do the things that will make your presence in my life grow. Help me to set up a time of Bible study and prayer daily and to discipline myself to fellowship with believers at church. I really do want my life to have more of you and less of me. Amen.

Scriptural Reference:

John 3:30

He must become greater; I must become less.

From Ordinary to WOW!

I Corinthians 1:26-31

Iron Chef America is one of my favorite television shows. During each episode, two chefs compete using a secret ingredient. Most often as not, the secret ingredient is ordinary every day fare; fish, chicken, potatoes, tomatoes or citrus fruit. However, what is created from these ordinary foods is magnificent!

It isn't the complexity of the ingredients that makes the dishes special; it's the expertise, talent and abilities of the master chef. The chef knows exactly what methods to use and what spices to combine to create magnificent dishes out of ordinary foods.

The same principle applies to our lives. We are ordinary people with incredible potential in the masterful hands of an almighty God. With unimaginable knowledge, our Lord combines life experiences to create followers, laborers, teachers, lay leaders, ministers, missionaries and evangelists.

God also uses students, employees, parents, executives, business owners, medical personnel, soldiers, police and fire persons, neighbors----the list is endless. Every walk of life has opportunity when given to God to do whatever He determines to fulfill His marvelous plan to save a lost and hurting world.

How do we become what God has intended us to be; by yielding ourselves to the work of the Holy Spirit in our daily circumstances. The Word says all things work together for our good—according to His plan. (Romans 8:28)

When we realize our potential through Christ, we understand that God can use us to do great things. It's not about what we can do; it's about what *God chooses* to do *with* us. God uses common people, like you and me, in combination with all the "ingredients" of life, to make something magnificent.

I Corinthians 1:26-31

Brothers, think of what you were when you were called. Not many of you were wise by human standards; not many were influential; not many were of noble birth.

But God chose the foolish things of the world to shame the wise; God chose the weak things of the world to shame the strong. He chose the lowly things of this world and the despised things—and the things that are not—to nullify the things that are, so that no one may boast before him.

It is because of him that you are in Christ Jesus, who has become for us wisdom from God—that is, our righteousness, holiness and redemption. Therefore, as it is written: "Let him who boasts boast in the Lord."

Prayer:

Lord Jesus, show me through your Word how to know your plan for my life. Confirm in my heart by your Holy Spirit your direction for my daily activities. I want my life to glorify you in all my choices. Thank you for being part of my life. Amen.

Scriptural References:

Romans 8:28

And we know that in all things God works for the good of those who love him, who have been called according to his purpose.

What's Your Flavor?

Philippians 2:12b-13

One of my grandsons loves Cookies 'N Cream ice-cream. His brother, on the other hand, prefers simple unadorned chocolate. Their sister embraces a mix of the two viewpoints. Sometimes, she prefers simple, other times, she prefers elaborate taste combinations. She says it just depends on how she feels that day.

God has made each of us different; different talents, different attitudes, family backgrounds, experiences, likes/dislikes and styles. We all have our own "flavor." The important thing is that we choose to love the Lord with all of our heart and seek only those things that please Jesus.

Being a Christian isn't about rules or regulations, it's about a relationship. When we have a personal relationship with Jesus, our lives and attitudes reflect that intimacy. As we grow in Christ, our deepening intimacy is revealed in every area of our life.

No matter how much we want to; we can not change anybody but ourselves. But, we do *influence* the lives of those around just as <u>those around us influence us</u>. As we spend time in God's Word, make time for prayer and take time to spend in fellowship with God's people, we become more and more Christ like.

<u>Philippians 2:12b-13</u>

"...work out your salvation with fear and trembling; for it is God who is at work in you, both to will and to work for *His* good pleasure"

<u>Prayer</u>:

Lord, help me to always realize that you created each of us in your own image and that you love each of us individually. You did not instruct us to go out and make disciples of ourselves, but rather disciples of you. Help me to know you intimately so that others see you in me. Amen.

The Fiery Hot Surprise

Ephesians 6:14-18

My grandson, Max, and I were at Subway ordering our lunch. After choosing his favorite meat and cheese for his sandwich, Max said, "Wait, one more thing; put ONE slice of jalapeno fiery hot pepper inside." The clerk looked at me for guidance; I shrugged, clueless.

The clerk asked, "Ok, so, just put it anywhere?" Max nodded, explaining when he ate the sandwich, "without warning, WHOP! There it would be; expected, but fiery hot and totally surprising!" Max shut his eyes tight, not seeing where the hot slice was placed and continued, "You just have to be ready so when it hits, you can get through it. It shakes you up but then, you go on.

In our lives, we have times when WHOP! Without warning, a fiery surprise hits us. Like Max, we knew that coming to that 'fire' would be a certainty, but when it actually hits, it takes our breath away. Our knowledge of who God is and what's really going on gets us through it.

Satan's number one goal is to rob us of intimacy with our Savior. No matter how well we live our Christian walk, 'fire' comes. God doesn't hurt us, sin and rebellion hurt us. Sometimes, we set the fire, sometimes, we get caught in the back draft of somebody else's fire. Regardless of how we find OUR fiery hot surprise, we must realize, we are not alone. Jesus even told his disciples that troubles were an everyday part of life. (John 16:33)

No matter how we get in the fire; we will choose what the personal result of the fire will be. Will we be angry and bitter or will we focus on Jesus, get through it and move on in Christ?

The devil hopes the 'fire' will destroy our life and our relationship. When fire comes, focus your eyes on Jesus and make it through. The fire can shake you up but it can't hurt your relationship with Christ unless you let it.

Ephesians 6:14-18

Stand firm then, with the belt of truth buckled around your waist, with the breastplate of righteousness in place, and with your feet fitted with the readiness that comes from the gospel of peace. *In addition to all this, take up the shield of faith, with which you can extinguish all the flaming arrows of the evil one.*

Prayer:

Lord Jesus, when the fiery trials of life come, help me to remember that these fiery times are a normal part of life. Show me how to overcome the fires and keep my eyes on you. Send me your Spirit to direct me and calm me. I love you, thanks for showing me how to walk through the fire. Amen.

Scriptural references:

John 16:33

"I have told you these things, so that in me you may have peace.[A] In this world you will have trouble.[B] But take heart! I have overcome[C] the world."

But Daddy Ate a Cookie

Proverbs 22:6

One afternoon, a young mom baked cookies to take to the PTA open house. As she left to run some last minute errands, she told her husband to not eat the cookies. She further instructed him to tell their son to not eat any when he got home from school as well; the cookies were for a meeting.

When mom came home the little boy was happily eating a cookie. She said, "I told your Daddy to tell you not to eat any cookies!" The little boy nodded, saying, "He DID tell me, but then after that, I saw him eating one so I took one too."

Children often learn a lot more through observation than what they are taught with words. "Do as I say not as I do" is not going to inspire anything but rebellion and a callous heart. Of course, as parents, we all make mistakes but that does not relieve us of our daily responsibility to try our very best to live the Christ life before our children and the world.

Choosing to follow in the footsteps of Godly parents is much easier than *choosing to follow God* ***in spite of*** what our parents taught us. Time and time again, in the Old Testament, God told the Israelites to not follow in their parent's footsteps in rebellion to God---yet, they chose to follow the rebellion anyway.

In Ezekiel 20:18, we read the words, "I said to their children in the wilderness, Do not follow the statutes of your parents or keep their laws or defile yourselves with their idols." It can be difficult to choose a different path when we have followed a wrong path since childhood---but God gives us strength to follow His ways.

Always be tender to the voice of the Holy Spirit and quick to back up if you find yourself out of step with Godly principals. The quiet voice of the Holy Spirit reminds us of our leadership role in parenting. God will show us how to correct the mistakes we have made IF we humble ourselves, admit our mistakes and walk on in Christ. Missteps made in front of our children can be made right, through an example of repentance, Bible study, prayer and commitment.

We teach by example when we listen with willing hearts and change our own lifestyle and choices to line up with Biblical principles. The most important thing we can do for our kids is show them Christ in our everyday life. We teach what we "know" but our kids learn the Christ life from watching how we actually live.

Just as you and I must make a personal decision to follow Christ or not, so must our children. If our own parents did not set an example for us, then we must turn our face to God and set a right example for our children so the heritage of rebellion will be ended.

Proverbs 22:6

Train a child in the way he should go and when he is old he will not turn from it.

Prayer:

Lord Jesus, please give me wisdom to make right decisions for my family. Help me to understand how little things I do can make a big difference in the life of those that I love. Show me how to lead in Christ and set the example of Jesus in all of my attitudes, plans, relationships and activities. I love you and I thank you for the Holy Spirit and your Word to guide me. Amen.

Scriptural References:

Ezekiel 20:18

I said to their children in the wilderness, "Do not follow the statutes of your parents or keep their laws or defile yourselves with their idols.

Potato Maintenance

James 4:4

Today I discovered that my bag of potatoes contained one rotten spud. Having heard the old analogy about "one bad spoils the whole basket," I decided to do an experiment.

Over the next several weeks, I made numerous observations about my sack of potatoes. The analogy turned out to be true. When a rotten potato was left against a good potato, in time; the good veggie started developing rot.

Interestingly, when the good potato was washed and dried everyday it did <u>not</u> develop the rot. Although, only with ***daily*** washing did the good spud continue to be good. However, being with the good potato still didn't make the bad one change to good. The only way the bad vegetable became good was to clean it, remove the bad spots and quickly involve it in a recipe.

If we make worldly people our constant companions, we can be influenced by their worldly ways. It is much easier for a Christian to take on the characteristics of the world than for the world to take on the attributes of Christ. (Jeremiah 17:9)

Whenever we fellowship with an unsaved friend, we need to make note of where we are in our personal relationship with Christ. Through the blood of Christ, daily washing in the water of the Word in Bible study and fellowship with believers, we <u>can</u> maintain our walk with our Lord. (Romans 12:2 & I John 1:7)

But, only if we are diligent with the things of God can we maintain our own spiritual integrity. If we find ourselves spending less time in prayer and Bible study and finding reasons to miss church, we need to recognize influence and step away from our "friend."

Simply being *with* a Christian doesn't make a sinner a Christian. The <u>only</u> way the friend will be saved is to become born again as a new creation. (II Corinthians 5:17) Should my friend resist my repeated efforts to be led to Christ; it is better to move away from my friend than to compromise my relationship with my Lord. Scripture confirms the influence that friends can have on our lives. (Proverbs 12:26)

It's important that I be <u>***truthful with my self***</u> as I look at my friendships. The influence of a friend can influence my relationship with Jesus. I must guard my heart and be consistent in Bible study and prayer. There *is* a difference between being a witness for Christ and being friends with the world.

James 4:4

You adulterous people, don't you know that friendship with the world is hatred toward God? Anyone who chooses to be a friend of the world becomes an enemy of God.

Prayer:

Father, God, help me to be diligent in Bible study and conversation with you so that my eyes and my heart recognize sin. Make me aware of every opportunity to lead those around me to salvation. Show me how to influence them to follow Christ and keep me sensitive to your Spirit so I'm aware if their influence begins to harm me. Amen.

Scriptural Reference:

Jeremiah 17:9

The heart [is] deceitful above all [things], and desperately wicked: who can know it?

Romans 12:2

Do not conform to the pattern of this world, but be transformed by the renewing of your mind. Then you will be able to test and approve what God's will is his good, pleasing and perfect will.

I John 1:7

But if we walk in the light, as he is in the light, we have fellowship with one another, and the blood of Jesus, his Son, purifies us from all sin.

II Corinthians 5:17

Therefore, if anyone is in Christ, the new creation has come: The old has gone, the new is here!

Proverbs 12:26

A righteous man is cautious in friendship, but the way of the wicked leads them astray

Make Room For More Fruit!

Galatians 5: 22- 25

Wonder of wonders, I've found a diet tool that works for me! Instead of the empty calories found in sweets, I indulge in the vitamin and nutrient rich sweetness of fruit. Fruit is delicious, healthy and satisfying. Fruit is so satisfying that when I eat it regularly, my desire for not so healthy snacks is lessened.

The fruit of God's Spirit works the same way. When we actively determine to choose more of God, we are satisfied with the fruit His Spirit brings us. What I love about God is I can have more; as much as I want! As I make conscious life choices that keep me supplied with the "good fruits" of joy, peace and self control, I find there is more than enough good fruit to keep me satisfied.

However, this abundance of the fruit of the Spirit leads to a storage problem. As long as my heart and life are full of the world, there is little room for the fruit of the Spirit. When the storage space in my mind and heart is crowded, I get depressed, moody and ill tempered. The only answer there can be is to make more space for the good fruit.

When I ask God to show me my heart, I find that there is quite a bit of useless junk lying around, even though I didn't notice it before--. As I allow the unsatisfying junk food of the flesh, like anger, greed, impatience and selfishness, to be taken out; space will be made available to bring more of God's fruit in.

Just like it is my choice to reach for a piece of candy or a piece of fruit, it is my choice to yield to the discipline of the Holy Spirit or--not. Daily, I make the choice of what I fill my heart and mind with, the good fruit of the Spirit or the fruit of the world. Just like with healthy food choices, I make the decision to choose a healthy spiritual life. God doesn't force me to do anything. It's totally up to me.

Galatians 5: 22- 25

But the fruit of the Spirit is love, joy, peace, patience, kindness, goodness, faithfulness, gentleness and self-control. Against such things there is no law. Those who belong to Christ Jesus have crucified the sinful nature with its passions and desires. Since we live by the Spirit, let us keep in step with the Spirit.

Prayer:

Father, thank you for giving me the fruit of the Spirit to fill the empty places in my heart. Help me to always reach for the healthy things instead of the temporary sweetness of the world's pleasures. I love you. Amen.

WHO DID THAT?

Ephesians 6:12

My friend bought pizza for supper. Arriving home, she put the pizza on the kitchen table. Her husband wasn't home from work yet so she left the pie unopened. When she came back into the kitchen she noticed her husband still wasn't home and decided she'd best eat while the pizza was still hot.

Opening the box, she found a large slice missing. She was FURIOUS! Obviously, a pizza store clerk had taken a piece of her pizza before it even left the store! She called the pizza store and told them what had happened. They denied it and politely said that was impossible. No employee would EVER remove a piece of pizza from a customer's order!

Furious, she informed them that she had picked up the pizza, come straight home, alone, nobody was in the house but her and she was absolutely positive nobody had opened the box before she did. The ONLY explanation was that a hungry employee had taken the slice. The store manager continued to say that was impossible—but—since they believed in customer service, bring the pie back and they'd replace it, which they did.

Arriving back at the house with a new pizza, she went into the house and once more put the unopened box on the kitchen table. Her husband pulled into the driveway and walked in the house right behind her. Going straight to the table, he lifted the lid of the pizza box and in puzzled astonishment said, "Praise GOD, the pizza healed itself!"

He had come home earlier and realized as he walked in the house that he'd forgotten something at the office. Noticing the pizza box on the table, he grabbed a slice, closed the lid and left. She'd never known he was in the house. Needless to say, my friend returned to the pizza store, explained, apologized and paid for the "new" pizza.

So often, as Christians, we blame "somebody" for a misdeed, a hurt feeling or a perceived wrong. Sometimes, we stop going to a class, cease to serve in a ministry, leave a church, or even stop going to church all together. We are hurt, angry, frustrated, disappointed and fed up. These hurts and disappointments are real, not imagined.

The truth is, we attack the wrong enemy. Ephesians 6:12 says that we don't fight against flesh and blood. One of satan's goals is to ruin our relationship with other Christians, removing us from the support of the body of Christ. In time, our inner pain becomes a form of idolatry and we feel we are justified in our separation from God's people. We worship our disappointment, anger and emotional pain instead of God.

Without the encouragement of fellowship with the body of Christ, we eventually lose our intimacy with Christ himself. Don't be fooled; your pain does not come from people, or church or God. It comes from satan himself. Don't let satan rob you of the very thing Christ died on the cross to give you; relationship with God and with each other.

Ephesians 6:12

For our struggle is not against flesh and blood, but against the rulers, against the authorities, against the powers of this dark world and against the spiritual forces of evil in the heavenly realms.

Prayer:

Lord Jesus, help me to see past the moment and understand that satan wants to rob me of the strength of fellowship that can be found in church. Remind me that your blood shed on Calvary set me free from the bondage of broken relationships and hurt feelings. In Jesus name, amen.

Sandwich Power

James 5:16

Every morning, when my kids were in school, I packed them a lunch. Not just any lunch but a lunch covered with prayer. School, even then, was a place of worldly influence and often persecution for those who went to church. So, I took lunch box prayers <u>very</u> seriously.

As I fixed the lunches, I prayed over every part then once completed, I prayed over the bag itself. I prayed that God would touch their lives, give them direction and create in them a heart of worship.

Years later, my oldest son was home to visit. He was active in his church and having newly married, established a Christ centered home. As we were chatting, he asked me if I remembered a guy he went to school with. I told him no, I didn't remember this boy.

My son laughed and told me that he was <u>the kid that always stole his lunch from him</u> at school. (I wasn't aware this had gone on) When I asked if he ever got his act together, my son told me the guy was the worship leader at a church. As I remembered the prayers that had been prayed over the stolen lunch, I had to laugh. God is faithful, in ways we can't even imagine.

Sometimes, our prayers are evidenced by committed lives or changed circumstances. Other times, we stand in faith, knowing that God uses the hard things in our life to manifest compassion for others (II Corinthians 1:3-4).

Every prayer is an answered prayer. God never ignores the prayer of his children. However, God is sovereign; He does whatever is necessary to accomplish His perfect will in the lives of those who truly seek Him. (Proverbs 16:9)

Sometimes, God even uses "us" in unlikely ways to bring Godly influence into the lives of others. Cover every area of your children's lives with prayer. Even though we often don't see the miracles that our prayers have influenced; prayer always works.

James 5:16

Confess your sins to each other and pray for each other so that you may be healed. <u>The earnest prayer of a righteous person has great power and produces wonderful results.</u>

Prayer:

Lord Jesus, thank you that you hear every prayer that your children make. Thank you that no issue is too small to lay at your feet and that no issue is too large to trust you with it. Help me to remember that you are wise far beyond my imaginings and that I can trust you with everything in my life. Amen.

Scripture Reference

II Corinthians 1: 3-4

Praise be to the God and Father of our Lord Jesus Christ, the Father of compassion and the God of all comfort, who comforts us in all our troubles, so that we can comfort those in any trouble with the comfort we ourselves receive from God.

Proverbs 16:9

In their hearts humans plan their course, but the LORD establishes their steps.

It's the Bread Crumbs

Psalms 139: 23-24

One of my favorite children's stories was Hansel and Gretel. Not because it was about good overcoming evil. It was about the bread crumbs. The kids left a trail of bread crumbs. Even as a child, I could get lost in my own neighborhood. Study courses on memory improvement haven't helped. My mind is like a steel trap; once information is inside, it can't get out.

Whenever I go anywhere, I always mentally mark my path and then allow an extra 30 minutes to anticipated travel time to get "unlost." The most useful method of getting back on track is to turn around and go back to where I started from. So simple and it works every time.

First, I have to admit I've gotten off track, then, I go back to where I lost my way. Once back on the right path, I can hold my head high because I chose to start over instead of continuing in the wrong direction. Pride doesn't matter; the only thing that matters is that I make my way home before I get hurt.

In our Christian walk, it's the same way. Every now and again, we realize that somehow, we've gotten off track. We look around us and discover "this" isn't where we intended to be. No body ever wakes up one morning and makes a conscious decision to stop serving God. It's a gradual process, made one casual decision at a time.

We get caught up in our daily activities and serving God is what we intend to do—but—first, I have to do this, be here, go there--. Tomorrow, I'll start doing my devotions again. This Sunday, I'll start going to church again. Each day, it gets easier to keep on our "new" road. In time, our new road is the familiar road and we look back less and less.

Right now, let's stop and look behind us. Are we faithful in keeping our daily conversation time with God, do we fellowship with Godly people, does our lifestyle reflect Christ? Or can we look behind us and see we've slowly lost our way? If so, turn around now, go back the way you came and get back on track.

Psalms 139: 23-24

Search me, O God, and know my heart; test me and know my anxious thoughts. See if there is any offensive way in me and lead me in the way everlasting.

Prayer:

Lord Jesus, please forgive me if I've lost my way. Give me a tender heart so I can hear the voice of your Holy Spirit and know how to keep my path straight. Help me to be aware of life's little side trips so that I know to keep my eyes on you. I love you. Amen.

Sometimes, It's All About me!

John 1:12

My grandson, Max, was the only one at school today; his brother and sister were sick. When I picked him up after school and asked how he was, he grinned from ear to ear and said, "I'm just GREAT! This morning, I had Mom *all to myself*."

He proceeded to tell me about his extravagant morning of individualized attention. He said usually in the morning, his mom is all about getting stuff ready and he gets cold cereal or something microwaved out of a box.

But this morning, with both his brother and his sister in bed with fevers, and his mom off work to take care of them, it was, and I quote, "all about Max." He said "Mom was all over me. She was saying, 'Maxie, do you need anything? Maxie how are you doing, are you ready to go yet?'"

He further revealed that breakfast this morning had been HOMEMADE FRENCH TOAST with *hot* syrup, not just syrup out of the bottle, served to him *personally*. He said he didn't have just one piece, but as many as he wanted! He declined to say how many pieces that was.

As we turned into his neighborhood, he leaned back in the seat and sighed, "Tomorrow, if I'm still the only one well, I'm gonna ask for some bacon to go with my French toast--." In today's busy world, individual attention is always a special treat!

One of the many things that I love about being a Christian is that our God cares for us personally. Even though God's grace is extended to all people, it requires an individual response to His invitation. Once I respond to this invitation for relationship, God's Holy Spirit brings me intimacy and "God" becomes MY God.

We are created for personal relationship with God but satan does everything he can to spoil that intimacy with our Lord. When Jesus hung on the cross, He was paying the *individual*, personal price for my sin. It was, "All about ME.

John 1:12

To all who received Him, to those who believed in His name, He gave the right to become children of God.

Prayer:
Lord Jesus, thank you for loving me so much that you died on the cross to pay for my sins. Help me to fully understand how much you love me. I accept your payment for my sins and ask you to help me to live for you every day. Amen.

Mine Has to Be BOLD!

Psalms 104:1-5

Being a lover of good strong "full bodied" java, the write ups in coffee advertisements using terms like, "flowery" amuse me. Do I choose a coffee because it teases my senses like a fresh cut flower? Am I looking for a morning cup that could be used as cologne?

NO! I don't want a cup of wimpy coffee. I like my coffee to be downright BOLD! In the same way, I'm the type of person who needs a bold God. My God has to be **ALMIGHTY**!

My God is not a god whose name can be used as a generic cuss word. My heart breaks for people whose god is so wimpy that they can say, "My god, it's hot outside." Seriously? Your god is so ordinary you can use his name to describe the weather? Why on earth is he your god if he's that common?

That's why I've chosen to serve the King of Kings, the Lord of Lords. He is the Alpha and Omega, the creator of the universe. Jesus Christ, the Lord God Almighty is my God. Who is YOUR God?

Psalms 104: 1-5

Praise the Lord, O my soul. O Lord my God, you are very great; you are clothed with splendor and majesty. He wraps himself in light as with a garment; he stretches out the heavens like a tent and lays the beams of his upper chambers on their waters. He makes the clouds his chariot and rides on the wings of the wind. He makes winds his messengers, flames of fire his servants. He set the earth on its foundations; it can never be moved.

Prayer:

My Lord, you are very great and holy. My heart is humbled by the understanding that you could love me so much that you want to spend time with me, to talk to me, to listen to me. Thank you that you have chosen me to be your child. I love you. Amen.

Exodus 20:7

You shall not misuse the name of the LORD your God, for the LORD will not hold anyone guiltless who misuses his name.

When Life Hands You Taco Meat

Romans 8:28

One night, as the kids were getting ready for bed, my grandson, Max, handed his mom a folded up piece of paper. In explanation, he told her that his teacher had sent "this" to her. He didn't remember exactly *when*, but maybe last Monday or the Monday before that—and he-- forgot.

She unfolded the paper and began to read. "Dear Mom, Thank you so much for volunteering to season, cook and bring to class six pounds of ground beef for Taco Day *Friday*" (tomorrow). Of course, she did what any mom would do, she gasped, "WHAT? I DID **WHAT**? WHEN DID I SAY I'D DO ***THAT***?!"

Max very confidently said, "Mom, I knew it wouldn't be any trouble for YOU. You make GREAT taco meat, that's why I said you'd do it." With that he hugged her and ran off to bed leaving the "great Taco meat cooker" making an unplanned trip to the grocery store in the middle of the night.

Especially when we are raising our families, we can have things that surprise us. Even when we are faithful to follow God's word and love Him, unexpected "stuff" can still happen. Sudden financial set backs, unexpected medical bills, car repair; the list can often be overwhelming.

It is good to know that before I'm even aware that I have a need, God has set actions in motion to meet that need. Sometimes, the need is not met the way I think it should be met. Sometimes there can even be important things that God plans for me to learn through that "need."

These life surprises can have consequences that alter our plans, our goals and even our lives. God also uses events in our lives as tools to work His will in the lives of others. None of life's events or circumstances catches God by surprise. If we are "in it" God has already planned a way for us to cope, even grow, through it.

Sometimes, God teaches us how He provides for us. Other times, He shows us how great His mercy is. And now and then, "taco meat" simply --just – happens. Through all of those times, trust and hold on to Jesus.

Be assured that God's plan is always at work in our lives to make us into the vessel He intends for us to be. Seek God's wisdom to handle daily struggles. The only way for handling life's surprises is through a relationship with Jesus.

Romans 8:28

For we know that in all things works for the good of those who love him, who have been called according to his purpose.

Prayer:

Father, help me to always remember to trust your handling of my life. Even through the difficult times, show me how to draw close to you and grow in your grace. Amen.

The Talking Bread

Isaiah 45:11

The soft rolls done and on the rise, I started working on making French bread. As I kneaded the dough, I was praying for friends and loved ones to be saved, healed, and their lives made easier.

Not just praying but giving *directions*, "God, get my brother THAT job and make the loan on THAT house come through for my friend." I was deep in prayer while I was vigorously kneading that French bread.

Mid-prayer, God questioned me, "What would you think if the dough spoke to you and said, "I think you should use a lighter hand to knead me so the bread will be more tender."

Startled, I told God, "French bread has to be kneaded with a heavy hand in order for the crust to develop properly; obviously the dough has no idea what I'm doing." God replied, "Even so." I stopped kneading, "What?????"

Then, I realized it wasn't up to me to tell God HOW to do things; it was my place to simply give the "life dough" of those I love to Him and let him "knead" as

He wills. My job ended at bringing their name before Him daily and praying that they be yielded to the Master's hand.

HE would decide what should be done to lead them, bend them or even break them. The circumstances and trials of their life were between Him and THEM. A plan for their individual lives as well as the lives of others <u>through</u> them had been made in full knowledge of the “dough” He was working with.

Like Joseph in prison; in the end, Joseph was exactly where God wanted him to be, to do exactly what God had planned for him to do. The “kneading” had been rough, but the finished loaf was perfect. God worked not only in Joseph’s own life but through his life to the nation of Israel.

Somehow, I’d been thinking that praying meant helping God out with decisions about the lives of others. I’d forgotten that God often uses diversity as a tool and as a witness. Now, I daily bring those I love to the Lord and---just leave them there-- with no direction or opinion given.

<u>Isaiah 45:11</u>

This is what the LORD says— the Holy One of Israel, and its Maker: “Concerning things to come, do you question me about my children, or give me orders about the work of my hands?"

Prayer:

Father, please forgive me for trying to tell you what to do in the lives of others. Help me to remember that you are a sovereign God who does not need to be instructed. Do as you will in the lives of those that I love so that your perfect plan will be realized. In Jesus' name. Amen.

Supper Always Shows Up

Luke 12:24

Our youngest daughter had a minor medical procedure done and had to "take it easy" for the rest of the day. That evening when she had returned home to her family, I took supper over to them.

Little 6 year old Dalton met me at the door and asked me what I was doing at his house. I told him I'd brought supper. His face lit up and he started jumping up and down laughing and dancing and yelling, "We ARE gonna get supper! We ARE!"

In his little boy mind, he had made note that his mama wasn't feeling well. There was nothing in the oven and he knew that his Daddy wasn't coming home till late. So, he just figured he was out of luck, no supper tonight!

God's plan <u>often</u> does not fit into our "box." He provides for us in a way we don't anticipate. When our need is great, we often can't imagine how it could be met. We dutifully pray; hoping for a miracle but accepting our plight as one of those things in life that may just have to be, "handled."

We expect nothing because the possibility of "something" is so unlikely. Then, we are surprised when; simply, with no fanfare, supper shows up! (John 21:3-6) God answers our prayers again and again, yet, we are astonished. (Acts 12:6-16)

God cares for every area of our lives; He has a plan for provision for our needs. Whether through ordinary ways that we just didn't think of, or through miraculous intervention, God always makes a way. Trust Him.

Luke 12:24

(Amplified Bible) Observe and consider the ravens; for they neither sow nor reap, they have neither storehouse nor barn; and [yet] God feeds them. Of how much more worth are you than the birds!

Prayer:

Father, thank you for always being on time when I need intervention in my circumstances. Forgive my doubt and help me to be confident that even though my need may not be met the way I anticipate, it will be met. Thank you for loving me and taking care of me. Amen.

Scriptural References:

John 21:3-6 '

I'm going out to fish,' Simon Peter told them, and they said, 'We'll go with you.' So they went out and got into the boat, but that night they caught nothing. Early in the morning, Jesus stood on the shore, but the disciples did not realize that it was Jesus.

He called out to them, 'Friends, haven't you any fish?' 'No,' they answered. He said, 'Throw your net on the right side of the boat and you will find some.' When they did, they were unable to haul the net in because of the large number of fish.

Acts 12:13-16

Peter knocked at the outer entrance, and a servant named Rhoda came to answer the door. When she recognized Peter's voice, she was so overjoyed she ran back without opening it and exclaimed, "Peter is at the door!"

"You're out of your mind," they told her. When she kept insisting that it was so, they said, "It must be his angel." But Peter kept on knocking, and when they opened the door and saw him, they were astonished.

Sin Is Like a Wild Turkey

Galatians 5:19-23

One year my youngest son, Paul, told me not to thaw the turkey, he was going to go turkey hunting. The day before Thanksgiving, before the sun was even awake, he headed out to hunt.

Indeed, he DID bring home a turkey. I told him, "well done," I'd cook it when it showed up in my kitchen sink plucked and gutted; mama doesn't clean game. All smiles, he happily went outside with his hunting knife and the big bird.

An hour later, a scrawny bird carcass lay naked in my kitchen sink. The "big" turkey had been mostly feathers. I did cook the bird; it was tough, stringy and absolutely inedible! We had a ham as a "side" dish.

Paul had a great sense of humor; laughing and joking with us about the "lame game." It was crazy how fabulous that bird had looked compared to how pitiful and tough it was when it was on the plate; who knew?

Sin is like a wild turkey. When you first see it, it's all big, fluffy and tempting. Satan knows that our eyes are easily deceived (II Corinthians 11:14). But, when you get down to reality; there's nothing but tough gristle.

When we read the Bible regularly, we are familiar with satan's tricks and not so easily duped (II Corinthians 2:10-11). The Holy Spirit is faithful to whisper warnings to our heart so that even when our eyes are tempted, our heart knows better. (John 16:8-15)

Satan works hard to make us stumble; he hates the relationship we have available through Christ. When we are faithful in Bible study and daily conversation (prayer) with our Lord, we are less likely to yield to temptation. Those (hopefully) rare times we do stumble, God is faithful to help us stand back up. (I John 1:7-10)

The Word says that the works of satan through our flesh are obvious. Make time to read the Bible so even the subtle sins like anger and envy are easily recognized.

Galatians 5:19-23

The acts of the flesh are obvious: sexual immorality, impurity and debauchery; idolatry and witchcraft; hatred, discord, jealousy, fits of rage, selfish ambition, dissensions, factions and envy; drunkenness, orgies, and the like. I warn you, as I did before, that those who live like this will not inherit the kingdom of God.

Prayer:

Father, help me to recognize sin and turn away from it. Give me the strength to resist temptation and the heart knowledge to realize that sin looks inviting but in reality, is cruel and hard. In Jesus name, amen.

Scriptural References:

II Corinthians 11:14

And no wonder, for Satan himself masquerades as an angel of light.

II Corinthians 2:10-11

Anyone you forgive, I also forgive. And what I have forgiven—if there was anything to forgive—I have forgiven in the sight of Christ for your sake, in order that Satan might not outwit us. For we are not unaware of his schemes.

John 16:8-15

When he comes, he will prove the world to be in the wrong about sin and righteousness and judgment: about sin, because people do not believe in me; about righteousness, because I am going to the Father, where you can see me no longer; [11] and

"I have much more to say to you, more than you can now bear. But when he, the Spirit of truth, comes, he will guide you into all the truth. He will not speak on his own; he will speak only what he hears, and he will tell you what is yet to come. He will glorify me because it is from me that he will receive what he will make known to you. All that belongs to the Father is mine. That is why I said the Spirit will receive from me what he will make known to you."!

John 1:7-10

But if we walk in the light, as he is in the light, we have fellowship with one another, and the blood of Jesus, his Son, purifies us from all sin.

If we claim to be without sin, we deceive ourselves and the truth is not in us. If we confess our sins, he is faithful and just and will forgive us our sins and purify us from all unrighteousness. If we claim we have not sinned, we make him out to be a liar and his word is not in us.

----

*Sin Is Like A Wild Turkey is also included in the book, "Life Is Like Buffalo Breath;" a devotion book that features heartwarming stories and antidotes about pets and animals to illustrate Biblical truth. Available on Amazon.

The Process Can Be Rough

II Corinthians 4:16-18

Cooking or baking, when you look at only the process, is rough. To bake a cake, you take a wire whisk and beat the sugar into the eggs until both individual parts lose their identity. You no longer have sugar or eggs, but an amalgamation. Two different entities become one, each losing their original identity to become a completely different "one."

To tenderize meat, you use an instrument called a needler. A method whereby fine incisions are made in the meat by closely spaced, specially designed knives which cut the connective tissue. The result is melt in your mouth tenderness. The experienced baker and chef know that every step is a necessary part of the process no matter how tedious or brutal it seems.

In the same way, we sometimes look at the circumstances of our own life, or the life of somebody we love and we think that they (or we) are being brutalized by God's process. Feeling battered and bruised, we cry out to God, "Whyyyyyy?"

In the Old Testament, we see the patriarchs rising above hardship, tragedy and, sometimes, even their own shortcomings, to emerge as mighty people of God.

In the book of Job, we see a righteous man taken from prosperity to the depths of suffering and back to prosperity; illustrating God's sovereignty through circumstance. The New Testament saints were beaten, persecuted and lived in poverty so that the knowledge of Christ could be spread.

When we study the scriptures; there are far more references to overcoming, conquering, standing strong, working hard and being responsible than there are about comfort and abundance. Sadly, today's Christian is often more focused on the sweet rewards of serving God than the hard truth about everyday life.

Satan's goal is to separate me from my Lord. Whether the devil chooses the tools of temptation, sickness, circumstances or bitterness; his ultimate goal is to lessen my relationship with Jesus.

Make note that satan's success relies on <u>my</u> participation in his plans! When life is difficult; I <u>*choose*</u> whether I turn to my Lord *or* turn away. Satan can try to influence me but he can not control me. Serving God with all of my heart is a moment by moment decision.

We serve God faithfully, even through hard times, because we know satan's schemes and we choose to walk strong in Jesus. The events in our lives that hurt can come from various directions. Sometimes, I do things that cause my own pain, other times; somebody hurts me.

Now and then, circumstances just work against me and cause me discomfort. Walking strong means forgiving those who have hurt us (II Corinthians 2:9-11) and growing through those things that satan has meant to defeat us.

When bad things happen, God has a plan to turn even the worst circumstances to our favor. (Genesis 50: 18-20) God's plan is to use everything that happens in our life to work to our good. Romans 8:28 doesn't say everything that happens in our life will feel good at the moment. But, rather that all things work FOR our good.

More importantly, life isn't just about "here, now." Life is a preparation for eternity, where we will rule and reign with Christ— so, stand strong even when you feel like you have been beaten. Always remember, God, like the master baker, knows what it takes to make His creation----beautiful.

II Corinthians 4:16-18

Therefore we do not lose heart. Though outwardly we are wasting away, yet inwardly we are being renewed day by day. For our light and momentary troubles are achieving for us an eternal glory that far outweighs them all. So we fix our eyes not on what is seen, but on what is unseen, since what is seen is temporary, but what is unseen is eternal.

Prayer:

Lord Jesus help me to keep my eyes on the goal of eternity with you. Give me grace, wisdom and mercy to handle every situation and circumstance that comes against me so that in all my attitudes and ways, I honor you with my life. Amen.

Scriptural References:

II Corinthians 2:9-11

Another reason I wrote you was to see if you would stand the test and be obedient in everything. Anyone you forgive, I also forgive. And what I have forgiven—if there was anything to forgive—I have forgiven in the sight of Christ for your sake, in order that Satan might not outwit us. For we are not unaware of his schemes

Genesis 50: 18-20

His brothers then came and threw themselves down before him "We are your slaves," they said.

But Joseph said to them, "Don't be afraid. Am I in the place of God? You intended to harm me, but God intended it for good to accomplish what is now being done, the saving of many lives.

Romans 8:28

And we know that in all things God works for the good of those who love him, who have been called according to his purpose.

Whack It With a Stick

Matthew 26:41

While looking for a recipe to cook a venison roast, I found a recipe for fried frog legs. It began, "Make sure the frog has stopped kicking and is dead. If necessary, whack it with a heavy stick." Alllrighty then! Obviously one of the ways we know something is dead is that "it" doesn't move.

Sometimes we think that we have "killed" sin in our life only to find that the sin still kicks. There is no shame or guilt in *being tempted*. We are all tempted; Jesus, himself, was tempted in every way (Hebrews 4:15.) Sin happens when we *give in to the temptation.*

As a Christian, I wrestle with sin every day. God sends the Holy Spirit to convict of sin so that I'm aware of temptation (John 16:8.) Only through the blood of Jesus can I get victory over the temptation that could lead to sin.

Once I ask Jesus into my heart, sin has no control over me, *unless I let it.* The way I keep sin out of my life is to be diligent through Christ. I don't deny sin or say it isn't really tempting; if "this sin" comes to mind then I'm still susceptible to its lure. Ignoring temptation does not make it go away.

Where I mess up is when I fail to deal with the temptation. A physical/mental/emotional action must be made the moment the temptation happens. The first thing I must do is make sure the sin is dead in my heart----by asking Jesus to forgive me. When temptation returns, the Holy Spirit will remind me that sin was put to death at Calvary and show me a way of escape.

There's no way within myself that I can win over temptation. If the temptation keeps kicking, I "whack it" with the heavy stick of God's word. I Use a concordance to find the scriptures that apply to "this" temptation—memorize them—and use as necessary. Only through the continuing study of God's Word and an intimate relationship with Jesus can I resist the wiles of the devil.

Matthew 26:41 Watch and pray so that you will not fall into temptation. The spirit is willing, but the body is weak.

Prayer:

Father God, thank you so much for showing me through your Word that Jesus understands how it feels to be tempted. Help me to realize that one of the Holy Spirit's jobs is to convict me of sin so that I can be aware of temptation. Give me strength to turn aside and not give in. Thank you. Amen.

Scripture References:

Hebrews 4:15

For we do not have a high priest who is unable to empathize with our weaknesses, but we have one who has been tempted in every way, just as we are--yet he did not sin.

John 16:8

When he comes, he will prove the world to be in the wrong about sin and righteousness and judgment.

Froggy Food Facts

Frog legs are commonly served as a delicacy in French and Cajun cuisines. Frog legs are considered to be a healthy food; rich in protein, omega-3 fatty acids, vitamin A and potassium. Cook to the same temperature required for cooking chicken.

Be God's Tool

II Timothy 2:23-24

This morning, I made wheat bread with dried cranberries, chopped English walnuts and cinnamon. Also, I made oatmeal cookies with those same ingredients. Both recipes also included flour, butter and salt.

The obvious question is, how could the same ingredients produce two such completely different outcomes? The outcome depends on the measure of the ingredients, the tools used in preparation, the method applied, the oven temperature and the subtle differences between the two recipes. In the end, it's ALL good.

In the same way, God uses our individual life circumstances to mold us into the vessel He has planned for us to be. As Christians, we are each created in the image of God, saved by the blood of Christ and endued with power by the Holy Spirit to worship God and serve as His disciples.

Paul addressed the sameness and the differences of individuals in the body of Christ in I Corinthians

12:21,"The eye cannot say to the hand, "I don't need you." And the head cannot say to the feet, "I don't need you." He emphasizes that even though we are each different, we are <u>all part of the same body</u>. Just as kitchen tools each have their own use, each individual in the church has a place of usefulness.

Satan's tactic is to divide and conqueror (Ephesians 4:25-27). First, he pulls me away from fellowship with unfounded feelings of inferiority. Then, he tells me that I'm not important and why even go to church, nobody needs me anyway. He acts as a giant spoon, stirring and stirring until everybody is comparing themselves to everybody else!

When we are focused on each other instead of the ministry God has called each of us to do, the body of Christ suffers. Discord and discontent tear down relationships. When we are angry with each other, our prayers are hindered and our ministry is ineffective (Matthew 5:23-24).

Satan works hard to stir up trouble in the body of Christ. My responsibility is to guard my heart to make sure <u>I'm</u> used as a tool for God, not satan.
<u>II Timothy 2:23-24</u>

Don't have anything to do with foolish and stupid arguments, because you know they produce quarrels. And the Lord's servant must not quarrel; instead, he must be kind to everyone, able to teach, not resentful.

Prayer:

Father, help me to be useful in your plan. Remind me that I'm an important tool created for your use. Forgive me for my feelings of annoyance and discontent. Help me to build and create instead of tear down and destroy. Show me how to be useful in your hands. Amen.

Scriptural References:

I Corinthians 12:21

The eye cannot say to the hand, "I don't need you!" And the head cannot say to the feet, "I don't need you!"

Ephesians 4: 25-27

Therefore each of you must put off falsehood and speak truthfully to your neighbor, for we are all members of one body. "In your anger do not sin" Do not let the sun go down while you are still angry, and do not give the devil a foothold.

Matthew 5:23-24

Therefore, if you are offering your gift at the altar and there remember that your brother or sister has something against you, leave your gift there in front of the altar. First go and be reconciled to them; then come and offer your gift.

============= ========== =============== ====

A Faith note: In the New Testament the apostles handed out prayer cloths (Acts 19:11-12). The scripture says that we should pray without ceasing and the prayers of a Christian accomplish much. What if we view meal preparation as a ministry opportunity? Every meal becomes a blessing and an opportunity—be God's tool.

==

Like I Ache For Cake

Psalms 63:5

The other day, I baked an extraordinary German Chocolate Cake. I'd toasted the pecans and the coconut before I put them in the special icing. It was, beyond any doubt, the most delicious German Chocolate Cake I'd ever made, bar none.

Later that night, I was lying in bed, when I remembered those layers of chocolaty sweetness; enrobed in a blanket of sweet coconut and toasty pecans. Once my mind started thinking about that cake, it's ALL that I could think of. I wanted a piece of that cake so bad; it was like an ache in the back of my throat! Mercy!

The Psalmist, David, wrote in Psalm 63:5 that his longing for God was satisfied like his body is satisfied with fine food. What an illustration! Thankfully, unlike aching for a piece of cake, the desire for intimacy with God is a good thing that has no down side to be regretted later.

In Psalm 34:8, David said, "Taste and see that the LORD is good." To be so intimate with the presence of God that you recommend that others "taste" it; what an incredible place to be. I love it when the Word uses everyday experiences to illustrate spiritual truth.

God longs for intimacy with us so much that He sent His only son to die so we could know Him. (John 3:16) But, wait, there's more! God sent His Holy Spirit so we could have not just a relationship but <u>intimacy</u> with Him. We were created not to just "know" who God is but for *personal* relationship.

There is no other god who wants a <u>*relationship*</u> with us! Out of that personal intimacy comes an awareness of who He is. We can't help but to worship in acknowledgement of the King of Kings, the Lord of Lords, the Great and Almighty God.

The more time I spend with the Lord through prayer and Bible study, the more I long for more of Him. Like when my throat aches for cake; when I think of my Lord, my throat aches to praise Him!

Psalms 63:5

My soul will be satisfied as with the richest of foods; with singing lips my mouth will praise you.

Prayer:

My Lord, you are a great and mighty God. I can't even imagine how you love me so much that you want to spend time with me, to talk with me. Help me to never forget what an honor it is to be in your presence, to read your Word and to be loved so completely. I love you and thank you. Amen.

Scripture References:

Psalm 34:8

Taste and see that the LORD is good; blessed is the one who takes refuge in him.

John 3:16

For God so loved the world that he gave his one and only Son, that whoever believes in him shall not perish but have eternal life.

BIG Very BIG

Jeremiah 10:6

At a community social event awards were being given and a reception was to follow. From my seat on the far side of the auditorium, I could see the cake across the stadium. It was sitting on a table many hundreds of yards away.

Obviously it was a big cake, because I could see it clearly from that great of a distance. But it didn't look like a seriously very large cake. I made a mental note that a lot of people were going to go home---cake-less. Or, perhaps, they had a few large sheet cakes sitting aside.

After the ceremony, I got in line to get my slice of the confection. I hoped they had another cake hiding somewhere in the back because the dessert I'd seen wasn't going to feed half the people, much less all the guests. Then, as I moved closer to the area where the dessert was, I discovered the cake was----HUGE.

It stood as tall as my head and was so big around I couldn't reach around it, not even if I held hands with a couple of friends! It was not sitting on a table, as I'd originally thought, but rather on a special platform that had been constructed to look like a table.

When in the auditorium, I'd viewed the cake from a great distance and it had looked small. When I stood closer to the confection, its actual size was revealed. Sometimes, it seems like God is small ---because where we're standing makes God look small.

The Children of Israel had a name for God that shows how BIG He is, Yahweh (Jehovah). The Hebrew meaning of the word is, "He who is at one with the limitless, unbounded universe because He has created it." Wow, that is quite—a description of our Lord.

The word, name, Yhwh, (Tetragrammaton) with this particular BIG meaning, is in the Bible only four times. (Exodus 6:3, Psalms 83:18, Isaiah 12:2 and Isaiah 26:4) The Jewish people held that BIG name for God in such respect that some claim that it was spoken just once a year and then only when they were in the temple at Jerusalem.

They believe that "BIG God name" is so Holy that they won't even write it down; using only symbols to represent it. They would *not even say that word in prayer* because it was so Holy!

God, Himself, in all of His magnificence and glory, was defined by that one name. Yet, that powerful, unwrite-able, unspoken—name, was, in their eyes, not adequate to describe the greatness of God.

Sometimes, because we're so busy with work, family, life, even church, we stand at a distance and don't see how BIG God really is. Situations and circumstances that I have no control over seem so huge because I have placed "that" *between* God and me.

According to scripture, God is so BIG that when he approaches, the mountains tremble (Nahum 1:5) He created the universe and calls the stars by name. (Isaiah 40:26)

My God is so magnificent that He wraps Himself in light, as if the light was a garment to be worn. The clouds are his chariot and He rides on the wings of the wind. (**Psalms 104:1-3)**

As I move in closer to my Lord, the problem doesn't change, but *my point of view does*. How BIG do I allow God to be in my life? It's up to me. How close do I want to get?

Jeremiah 10:6 No one is like you, O LORD; you are great, and your name is mighty in power.

Prayer:

My Lord, you are very great, you created the universe and call the stars by name. Help me to focus on your power and strength when I'm afraid. Help me to accept your sovereignty over every circumstance and simply ---trust you. Thank you for your faithfulness. Amen.

Scriptural References

Exodus 6:3

I appeared to Abraham, to Isaac and to Jacob as God Almighty, but by my name the LORD I did not make myself fully known to them.

Psalms 83:18

Let them know that you, whose name is the LORD, that you alone are the Most High over all the earth

Isaiah 12:2

Surely God is my salvation; I will trust and not be afraid.The LORD, the LORD himself, is my strength and my defense he has become my salvation

Isaiah 26:4

Trust in the LORD forever, for the LORD, the LORD himself, is the Rock eternal.

Nahum 1:5

The mountains quake before him and the hills melt away.The earth trembles at his presence, the world and all who live in it.(

Isaiah 40:26

Lift up your eyes on high And see who has created these stars, The One who leads forth their host by number, He calls them all by name; Because of the greatness of His might and the strength of His power, Not one of them is missing.

Psalms 104:1-3

Praise the LORD, my soul. LORD my God, you are very great; you are clothed with splendor and majesty. The LORD wraps himself in light as with a garment; he stretches out the heavens like a tent and lays the beams of his upper chambers on their waters. He makes the clouds his chariot and rides on the wings of the wind.

Do WHAT?

I Corinthians 2:10-12

Even now, as an experienced cook, I sometimes have to look up a cooking term. A good cook is never shy about asking about or looking for a word to find out what it means.

Making bad food can often be easily avoided by taking a minute to look a strange word or direction up. The quest for knowledge is lifelong; there will never be a time when a good cook knows enough that they can stop learning. Just saying.

In the same way, when I study God's Word, and I read something that I don't understand, the first thing I do is pray, asking God to send His Holy Spirit to teach me and lead me to truth. Then, I research the words out and read the verse in several different translations.

It is also helpful to make sure that I know the History of the time the verse was written, the contents of the chapters surrounding the chapter I'm reading and some background on the book of the Bible I'm reading. The Bible is rich in History and a fascinating read.

It is intriguing to read the Bible, learning that people are people, whether in ancient times or modern. We are tempted, tried, suffer the same afflictions, the same attitudes---only the setting and customs have changed. No matter what difficulty I face, God's Word not only has answers, but when applied diligently, gives me the power to change my attitudes, heart and my life. (Hebrews 4:12)

Each time I read it, I learn something knew as the Spirit leads me (II Timothy 3:16-17). God gives us His Spirit so that we can have intimacy with our Lord, and know His direction.

I Corinthians 2:10-12

--these are the things God has revealed to us by his Spirit. The Spirit searches all things, even the deep things of God. For who knows a person's thoughts except their own spirit within them? In the same way no one knows the thoughts of God except the Spirit of God. What we have received is not the spirit of the world, but the Spirit who is from God, so that we may understand what God has freely given us.

Prayer:

Father, you created me, you have searched me and you know me. There is no part of me that is hidden from you. Even my most distant thoughts are close to your ear. Please send me your Holy Spirit to teach me, direct me and teach me your ways. Give me listening ears to know your plan for my life. Give me a tender heart so that I know your voice and your great love for me. I love you. Thank you for loving me enough to instruct me. Amen.

Scriptural References

Hebrews 4:12

_For the word of God is alive and active. Sharper than any double-edged sword, it penetrates even to dividing soul and spirit, joints and marrow; it judges the thoughts and attitudes of the heart.

II Timothy 3:16-17

All Scripture is God-breathed and is useful for teaching, rebuking, correcting and training in righteousness, so that the servant of God may be thoroughly equipped for every good work.

Get Your Mess in Place

2 Timothy 2:15

There is a cooking term that, when understood, will help any recipe you make come together smoothly. *Mise en place* (pronounced MEEZ-ahn-plahss). It's French and it means, in common English terms, "to put in place" or "put everything in its place." Being a simple person who has never been to France, never spoken French and at this point in life, I'm fairly certain I never will, I remember this term simply as, "Get Your Mess In Place."

French or not, this idea is a time saver and a head ache preventer. There is nothing more frustrating than being all ready to bake or make only to find out half way through the process, you don't have enough of one of the ingredients or that you loaned "that" pan to your cousin, Thelma. By "getting your mess in place" before you start, you will never suffer this frustration.

Planning a time for Bible study is a lot like planning a meal. You set a time to start preparing a meal because without a plan, supper doesn't happen. In like manner, plan a time to spend in Bible study and prayer.

Then, like getting ready to prepare supper, make sure you have your "mess in place" gathering all the tools you need, like a Bible that you can easily read, a paper pad and pen for taking notes, concordance and a devotional or Bible study book.

If you planned your meals the same way you plan your spiritual food, what kind of diet would you be eating? Don't just read a few Psalms every day and walk away feeling well fed. That's like eating dessert every night instead of meat and vegetables; you feel satisfied, but in the long run you will not be strong and healthy. It is important to study God's Word in its entirety so we grow strong and healthy spiritually. (II Timothy 3: 14-17)

As with a healthy diet, a healthy spiritual life requires discipline, planning and, of course, action. You can have a shelf full of great cookbooks, a cabinet full of the best equipment—but if you don't take the time to get all the ingredients and tools out and then actually ---use them. You go hungry.

Like any other life maintenance, study and conversation with others are very important. And of course, like you would share a recipe or tell your friends about a good meal, share your faith.

II Timothy 2:15

Do your best to present yourself to God as one approved, a worker who does not need to be ashamed and who correctly handles the word of truth

Prayer: Father God, thank you for sending me your Holy Spirit to help me study your Word. Show me how to organize my day so that I plan a time of Bible study with the same faithfulness that I do my every day routines. Thank you for wanting to talk to me and to listen to me. I love you. Amen.

Scriptural References:

II Timothy 3:14-17

But as for you, continue in what you have learned and have firmly believed, knowing from whom you learned it and how from childhood you have been acquainted with the sacred writings, which are able to make you wise for salvation through faith in Christ Jesus.

All Scripture is breathed out by God and profitable for teaching, for reproof, for correction, and for training in righteousness, that the man of God may be competent, equipped for every good work.

Got to TELL Somebody!

Mark 7:24

While grocery shopping the other day, I discovered that rib eye steaks were on sale. Buy one get one free. What an incredible bargain! I was SO excited about the good news that I called my friend, Celia, to share it with her so she could get some steaks too.

I didn't talk to her for very long because I wanted to call some other friends and let them know about the fabulous sale as well. An incredible good deal like THAT is simply too good to keep to myself.

This is how we should think about sharing the Gospel; so good we can't keep it to ourselves! It is human nature to share our triumphs.

The fact is, satan doesn't care if we tell our friends about a good sale; but, he <u>does</u> care when we share our testimony. *That's* why we feel so timid about sharing the Good News. That's why it's so hard to witness to our family and friends.

Satan works hard to make us feel stupid about sharing our faith. But, as Christians, we have the best news *ever*! Forgiveness of sin, direction for life, hope for healing and a *personal* relationship with the Lord God Almighty; all free, paid for at Calvary. Quite literally, we have the greatest news on earth.

Tell somebody about it! Witnessing is simply sharing good news with somebody who hasn't heard yet. Just like we'd be excited to share news of a great sale on steaks, we should have the same enthusiasm in telling our friends about Jesus. Something this great, we can't possibly keep it to ourselves!

Mark 7:24

Jesus left that place and went to the vicinity of Tyre. He entered a house and did not want anyone to know it; *yet he could not keep his presence secret.*

Prayer: Lord God, help me to be excited about salvation and your great love. Send me your Holy Spirit so the good news of the Gospel is always near to my lips so I can tell it boldly, as I should. Direct me to friends who need to hear about your great love. Amen.

Do I Want It My Way?

I Corinthians 2:14-16

Sitting at the stop light I notice a sign at a hamburger chain that generously states: "Have it your way." The thought came to mind; that sometimes, I have a burger attitude toward God. I want God's blessings in my life; I want His protection and direction. BUT, I want it on my own terms, I want it MY way.

God created me, He sent His son to walk as a man so that He has full understanding of everything I face in my lifetime. Jesus was tempted in every way that I can be tempted, but Jesus didn't sin (Hebrews 4:15).

As a human, Jesus had the option of doing things "His way" or God's way. (Luke 22:39-42) Reading the scripture, I realize that Jesus understands how tempting it is to opt for the easy way, "my way," instead of God's way.

Scripture also reveals that, when faced with the immediate relief of doing things the flesh way instead of the God way, Jesus told God about it; He CRIED OUT. He was in agony, recognized the temptation and instead of crumbling, He looked to God for strength. (Luke 22:41-44) The "God's way" decision was a *choice*.

Looking back over my life, I realize that the times I stepped out of God's will, it wasn't intentional; it was in desperation. Brought by my own humanity and the circumstances of life to a point of testing (James 1:13-14), instead of crying out to God for help and strength, I crumbled and gave into “my way.”

God's Word tells me that even when I slip and step over the line, doing things in the flesh; God is faithful to show me how to return to His way (I John 1:9). The Holy Spirit gives me the mind of Christ so I can understand the pain that going my own way can cause to both my Lord and those around me.

Whenever I’m faced with the decision of having life my way or God’s way, I’ll cry out to God and with the help of the Holy Spirit, I will choose God’s way.

I Corinthians 2:14-16 The natural person does not accept the things of the Spirit of God, for they are folly to him, and he is not able to understand them because they are spiritually discerned. The spiritual person judges all things, but is himself to be judged by no one. “For who has understood the mind of the Lord so as to instruct him?” But we have the mind of Christ.

Prayer: Lord Jesus, thank you for setting the example for me and sending me your Holy Spirit to give me direction to make Godly decisions. Help me to have strength to resist temptation and the wisdom to make right decisions. Thank you for caring so much for me. I love you. Amen.

Scriptural References:

Hebrews 4:15 For we do not have a high priest who is unable to empathize with our weaknesses, but we have one who has been tempted in every way, just as we are—yet he did not sin.

Luke 22:39-42 Jesus went out as usual to the Mount of Olives, and his disciples followed him. On reaching the place, he said to them, "Pray that you will not fall into temptation." He withdrew about a stone's throw beyond them, knelt down and prayed, "Father, if you are willing, take this cup from me; yet not my will, but yours be done."

Luke 22:41-44 He withdrew about a stone's throw beyond them, knelt down and prayed, "Father, if you are willing, take this cup from me; yet not my will, but yours be done." An angel from heaven appeared to him and strengthened him. And being in anguish, he prayed more earnestly, and his sweat was like drops of blood falling to the ground.

James 1:13-14 When tempted, no one should say, "God is tempting me." For God cannot be tempted by evil, nor does he tempt anyone; but each person is tempted when they are dragged away by their own evil desire and enticed.

I John 1:9 If we confess our sins, he is faithful and just and will forgive us our sins and purify us from all unrighteousness.

The following pages are excerpts from:

"Food for Soul AND Body"

A unique devotional cookbook that has the devotions you read in this book, PLUS favorite recipes of family and friends and some useful cooking tips. A perfect gift for your friends who love to cook AND a great cookbook for your own bookshelf.

Your Mise en place

The first thing you do is:

1) Read the entire recipe, start to finish. It is best to do this at least a day before you plan to make the recipe so you have time to shop for ingredients you don't have. Make a shopping list so you don't forget what you need and go get the missing ingredients. Also good to make sure you actually have the pans and utensils called for to make the recipe. Call your cousin and tell her you need your "special pan" back, you're coming over to get it---now.

2) Clear off your work area. I don't know about you, but I need SPACE when I cook.

3) Get all your stuff together. That means bowls, mixers, spoons measuring devices, knives, pans, paper towels, spices, etc.

4) Go through all of the ingredients in the order they appear in the recipe. Wash, peel, measure, and chop all the individual items as described in the recipe. Measure precisely, particularly if baking; baking is a lot about science and chemical reaction. Remember a tablespoon has a level top, it doesn't look like a mountain.

Some cooks like to put the ingredients on small plates or little cups or bowls so they are easy to handle. I like to put all the dry ingredients together so I have just one bowl of "dry" instead of a whole parade of little dishes. But, do whatever makes YOU feel "organized and ready."

5) Preheat oven if you are baking.

6) Start assembling the ingredients following the directions exactly. If you are an experienced cook, then you know how things go together, just get busy. If you are new to cooking, take a deep breath and take your time. It's going to be fine. Cooking is not a chore, unless you make it one. Look at it this way---everybody eats, so, cooking is simply-- a part of living.

7) Clean as you work. Keep a "garbage bowl" nearby to put peelings in. Place dirty containers in the dishwasher or sink. You will have enough time while pots are boiling and meats are searing or batter is beating or baking to clean up after yourself. If nothing else, it will make the cleanup when you're done go faster. The one thing I hate about cooking is---it makes such a mess. But, when I keep up after myself as I work, cleanup is much easier.

8) After you have cooked/baked the item in the recipe, take a moment to make a few notes about the finished dish. “Needs more (or less) salt.” Little comments in the margin of a recipe will help you make a recipe your very own.

Helpful Measurements

3 teaspoons = 1 tablespoon

4 tablespoons = 1/4 cup

5 1/3 tablespoons = 1/3 cup

8 tablespoons = 1/2 cup

12 tablespoons = 3/4 cup

16 tablespoons = 1 cup

1 tablespoon = 1/2 fluid oz.

1 cup = 8 fluid oz.

1 cup = 1/2 pint

2 cups = 1 pint

4 cups = 1 quart

2 pints = 1 quart

4 quarts = 1 gallon

Grandma's Smashed Potatoes

The Queen of comfort foods, the star of any holiday dinner, everybody loves "smashed potatoes!" This recipe makes enough smashed potatoes to feed 10-12 people. Or enough to feed 5 with leftovers for potato patties later (recipe at bottom of this recipe)

Ingredients:

5 pounds of Russets or Yukon Gold potatoes + 1 Tablespoon of salt

3 sticks of butter cubed (recommend you use real butter, not margarine)

1 1/2 cups of half and half (might not use it all depending on how thirsty the potatoes are)

1 1/2 cups of sour cream (you can substitute UNflavored GREEK yogurt for a lower fat content with no loss of flavor; I cut where I can without sacrificing yummy)

2 pounds of bacon chopped then crooked until crispy but not burned. (I often buy 1 pound of the pre-cooked bacon and just chop it up---saves a lot of

time and comes well drained of excess fat and does fine)

Salt and Pepper (taste test to see how much salt your family likes---it is a personal decision, some think boiling the potatoes in salted water adds enough flavor)

Instructions:

Boil the potatoes, skin and all with the salt in water to cover in large pan (if you don't like the peels, peel them first, I love the peels left on), until just fork tender. Don't over cook.

While the potatoes cook, combine butter, the half and half and the sour cream in a small pan or microwave safe dish. Heat just till warm—and keep warm till use because you don't want the milk products to make the potatoes cold when you add them.

Drain potatoes well and return to the pan over medium heat for a minute or two to remove all excess liquid. Stir or shake while doing this. When dry (sizzle stops) *remove from heat*, but leave in the pan they cooked in so they stay warm.

Smash the potatoes. (use a hand held masher, or a potato rice or an electric hand mixer, whatever YOU like to use) until smashed but do not over do it if you use a mixer or the potatoes will get gluey. These are old fashioned mashed potatoes and a little texture is good. Old fashioned smashed are not silky smooth.

Add the warm dairy products until you have the moisture you want, keeping in mind that the potatoes stiffen a little bit as they sit on the table. Taste for salt---some don't use any salt other than the salt in the water they cooked in, some like a lot—so taste and add salt till you "like" the flavor. Lastly, gently fold in the bacon till thoroughly incorporated. Heap high in a pre-warmed bowl (pour a cup of boiling water into the bowl, swish it around, dump the water out and thoroughly dry) Drop a dollop of butter in the top and sprinkle with pepper for that special "grandma's home made" look.

Potato Patties

If you're not feeding a dozen people smashed potatoes, you will have a good amount of left overs. Cover and refrigerate, keeps up two days.

Instead of just warming them up, add some chopped onion, one beaten egg and a tablespoon of self rising flour and mix together. (if mixture is too loose, add another teaspoon or two of self rising flour)

Scoop out with a large ice cream dipper into a hot non-stick skillet greased with a couple of tablespoons of butter or oil. With the back of a buttered spoon, spread the “lump” into a thick patty. Cover and cook over medium heat until brown and crisp on the outside and thoroughly heated on the inside. Turn once to brown both sides.

How to Eat a Cupcake
As explained by Pastor Jeff Overton

The cupcake is perhaps the world's only perfect dessert. It is the perfect size; easily held in only one hand allowing the other hand to remain free for your beverage.

You don't have to try and decide which piece of cake to choose. You are neither piggish nor picky; you simply have a cupcake-- just like everybody else.

Each individual cupcake is totally perfect, the same size and the same amount of icing. The decorations can be simple or extravagant, making it usable for casual treats or elaborate wedding celebrations.

Every cupcake is in its own cute little serving dish, which, by the way, is easily disposable. No clean up or dishwashing needed.

Such a perfect dessert has only one drawback. How many times have you opened your mouth to bite into a luscious cupcake only to realize you will end up with icing on your nose?

This is unacceptable when in the company of guests. Of course, when you are alone, you are free to dive in face first with no fear of humiliation by your peers.

If you try to bite into the sweet from the top, you risk knocking the icing off or getting all icing and little or no cake—leaving the remaining cake to be eaten without any icing at all. That is totally unacceptable.

How then, should a cupcake be eaten?

1. Remove cupcake wrapper.
2. Pull cupcake apart so you have 2 pieces of cupcake; the icing half and the cake half.
3. Turn icing half upside down so that icing is now in the middle, like a sandwich.
4. Now, you can enjoy your cupcake sandwich, each bite having both frosting and cake and no icing on your nose. Enjoy!

****

Every dish you prepare should always be anointed with prayer.

Strange cooking terms

Ahrs. The increments of time that measures how much actual time it takes to do something. Spare ribs take up to 6 ahrs, pulled pork can take up to 14 ahrs, etc.

Al dente. An Italian word that means roughly "to the tooth." What it means is that the food (like pasta or veggies) is not cooked until it is soft and squishy. Many people prefer al dente foods, many do not. It's a matter of what you like your food to feel like in your mouth---squishy---or firm.

Aromatic: What does a recipe mean when it calls for an "aromatic?" Aromatics are vegetables used to add flavor to a dish, such as onions, celery, carrots or shallots. Usually, the recipe tells you what to use then simply references those ingredients later on as "the aromatics."

Au jus. A gravy made from the natural drippings of the meat. Or "meat juice."

Bard: Bard is a weird cooking word that gives no clue to what it could be meaning. To bard is to cover meat with a thin layer of fat before roasting. Many folks today see this as NOT healthy cooking.

However, it is an excellent way to add moistness and flavor to lean meat.

What lots of folks fail to understand is that when you take the fat out of meat---you make it dry. In my humble opinion, I'd rather have a small portion of juicy "fatty" meat than a larger portion of healthy, tough, dry meat that makes my jaws ache to chew it. You decide for yourself, we all choose our battles. Of course, always follow your own doctor's dietary guidelines----.

Bark. The brown crunchy crust that forms on some foods, like smoked meats. It is mainly caused by seasonings from the rub, and dehydration of the meat's surface. Some people, like me, really like bark. Some hate it. It is a matter of mouth feel and taste. Bark can be hard, even crunchy.

Black & Blue. Red meat, like beef, grilled to the point of being almost charred on the outside, and "blue," which is a term for very rare, on the inside. Sometimes called "cooked to Pittsburgh."

Blanch: Foods are submerged in boiling water for a very short time, a few seconds to minutes but usually less than five minutes. Then they are quickly immersed in cold water. One reason for blanching is to cook a food just enough to loosen skins or peels to make them easy to remove, like the skins on peaches, plums and tomatoes.

Foods are also blanched to preserve their bright color like with green beans and asparagus, where the food is quickly immersed in boiling water then immediately removed to an ice bath (a bowl of cold water with ice in it) so germs are killed but the colors are made vibrant.

Blanching is also an important step in canning vegetables to kill bacteria before placing in glass jars or freezing. One of my childhood memories is of a huge pot of boiling water that my mom put bowls full of fresh green beans in---then took them right back out before filling canning jars.

Braising. A slow method of cooking, usually in reference to meats in thick stews. The food is usually not submerged in liquid. It is only partially covered in hot, but not boiling liquid for a long time, perhaps 6 to 12 hours. Braising is usually done in large pots (like a Dutch ovens or a crock pot) and the lid is usually not on tight. The result is a very tender, moist meat where everything in the pot contributes to the flavor.

Brine. A liquid that is very high in salt. Soaking some meats in a brine for an hour or more can add moisture and tenderness. Poultry and ribs are the meats most often brined. Often, herbs or seasonings are added to the brine, like garlic or cayenne pepper to add flavor.

Bruise: How do you get bruised? It is a similar concept when using "bruised" as a cooking term. To bruise is to crush, punch or pound in order to release flavor. Fresh herbs are often "bruised" to release their flavors. Particularly mint and basil are sometimes "bruised" in a recipe.

Butterflying. When you slice a large, thick pork chop or a large shrimp most of the way through but not all the way and spread open before cooking. Many times the "cavity" is filled with savory dressing or fruit then the meat is tied with twine to encase the filling. It is important to make sure the inside of the meat and the stuffing comes to a safe temperature before eating.

Capsaicin. The chemical in chili peppers that makes them taste hot. Most of the capsaicin resides in the ribs of the pepper with some in the seeds as well. When you want the flavor of a pepper but not the serious heat carefully, with a small sharp paring knife (wear gloves) carefully remove the ribs inside the pepper and the seeds. Rince the empty pepper in cold water. A bit of the heat may remain, but greatly reduced.

Caramelization. Most often to brown chopped onion till it releases its natural sugar giving it a rich, complex, caramel or butterscotch flavor. This must be done "low and slow." It takes at least 20 minutes to caramelize a pan of chopped onions. Believe me, it is worth the time and effort. As the onions brown, stir gently. If the process is not done over low heat with time, you just end up with cooked onions. Also the term can be reference to browning of meat.

Clarify: To clarify is to separate solids from liquids, making it clear. This process is often mentioned as applied to butter. When you put butter into a skillet or pan and melt it, the solid separates into a foamy white liquid that settles to the bottom (milk solids) and a clear yellow liquid. When you strain the solids out, just the yellow liquid, the "clarified" butter is left.

Collagen. The connective tissue that muscle sheathing is made from. When cooked this protein melts and forms a gelatin which gives meat a silky mouth feel. It is not something that can be added to a recipe. It is a substance found naturally in meat.

Cracklings or cracklins. Pig skin fried crisp. Can be used to season beans, potatoes and gravy. Tradition dictates they be either slow roasted on the barbecue or deep fried in lard.

Deglaze: Have you ever baked a roast, and planned to make gravy, but when the roast was removed from the oven, there was hardly any juice? To deglaze you would add water to the pan (after removing the roast), and scrape up the remaining bits that are left in the pan.

Dry-Aged Beef. The process of aging meat, particularly beef ribeye and strip steaks, in a temperature and humidity controlled environment. It sounds nasty, but, enzymes and molds work to dehydrate the meat and concentrate the flavors giving the meat a deep earthy flavor. Dry aged beef is hard to find, 28 days old is the most common age, and it is very expensive.

Dry-Cured Ham (also called Country Ham) is cured (preserved) by burying it in a big mound of salt or by rubbing the skin with large amounts of salt. Sometimes, the salt is mixed with sugar, black pepper, garlic, and other spices. In some places sodium nitrate is also added. After being heavily salted, it is usually hung and air-dried for 6 to 18 months at cool temperatures.

The meat dehydrates, concentrating its flavor. Often it is smoked at low temperatures as it dehydrates. It is usually served uncooked and sliced thin. It has a unique salty taste and the texture is very different than any other kind of ham. Because production takes a lot of time, dry-cured hams can be expensive. Virginia dry cured ham is very popular as a "country style" ham.

Emulsion. A blend of two liquids that don't want to blend, like oil and water. Salad dressings are the most commonly used emulsions in cooking because vinegar and vegetable oil separate quickly. They can be emulsified by shaking for a long time, or they can be made to stay mixed with an emulsifier like mustard. Xanthan gum is a common emulsifier in commercial food processing. So the next time you see the "Xgum" on the ingredients list, it isn't a useless additive, it has an important purpose—it keeps the ingredients from separating in the jar.

Eviscerate: This is not a term I like. To eviscerate is to remove the entrails of fish, fowl or other animals. I do not cook anything that isn't ready for recipe prep. However, if you are a cook that doesn't mind beheading, skinning, gutting and/or scaling; then good for you. I cook only meat that shows up looking like meat. Just saying.

Fond. Another French word, this one means the browned bits on the bottom of the pan after you sauté or pan fry things. It is full of yummy flavor and should not be left as throw away. By adding a few ounces of a liquid such as water, wine, or juice, keep the heat on high, quickly scrape the fond loose and dissolve it in the liquid. Use the dark liquid as the basis for a yummy pan sauce.

GBD. A cook's acronym for "Golden Brown and Delicious." Everything you cook should be GBD.

Glaze. A shiny coating. Glazes get their sheen from sugar and often times sauces are also glazes. Glazing something doesn't necessarily have to be a big process. You can simply brush honey or fruit juice on meat and it will make a yummy glaze. When baking "glaze" refers to a thin mixture of confectioners' sugar mixed with water or milk. Often used as a coating on fried pastry like donuts or as a "crumb catcher" brushed lightly on cake layers before icing.

Hoofta. An old time measuring reference used by old cooks. A hoofta is the amount it would take to fill the palm of your hand. In other words, a hoofta is a handful. Of course if granny has tiny or big hands---it could make all the difference in the outcome of the recipe. Best to use a measuring cup.

Hot 'n' fast. The opposite of low 'n' slow. Put the pot, pan or skillet on a high heat and make it screaming hot so when you add the food to be cooked it cooks fast, usually with crispy edges

Indirect heat. Cooking food by NOT putting it directly over the heat source so it can heat more slowly at a lower temperature. A double boiler uses indirect heat. (a pan placed over a pan of hot water---most often used to melt chocolate or blend eggs with a liquid so that the eggs don't scramble)

Jus. A gravy made from the juices of a meat with no other add ins. A jus means, "juice it was cooked in."

Low 'n' slow. The opposite of hot 'n fast. Cooked by keeping the heat low, under 250°F, sometimes even lower, and taking your time to cook it. The fat in the meat melts, making the meat juicy and flavorful. When you heat meat up too fast, the proteins can get bunched up in a knot and that makes meat.

Macerate: You might find a recipe that tells you to macerate the fruit in sugar or wine or lemon juice. Sounds crazy weird, doesn't it? It isn't, it just means to combine the fruit in the sugar, wine or lemon juice, lightly mash together, and then let stand to absorb the flavors.

Marbling. The white fat within the meat in a pattern so it looks, literally, like marble. The more marbling, the more tender, juicy, and yummy the meat tastes. To a great extent, the USDA meat grades for beef are determined by the amount of marbling. Shiny red meat cooks up dry and tough. When red meat lacks marbling, you can take a sharp knife and cut slits in the meat and stuff slices of chilled butter or suet into the slits.

Marinade. A liquid to soak the meat in to make it tender and flavorful. Similar to a brine, but with much less salt and more acid and oil. Both oil and acid (fruit juice, vinegar, wine) can make meat tender and add extra flavors. Sometimes an inexpensive piece of meat can be given extra "yummy" by marinating.

Meat glue. An invention of food science. Meat glue, listed on labels as transglutaminase (TG), is an enzyme that can bond proteins like glue. You know how when you are working with meat, it makes your fingers feel sticky? That's why it is called, "meat glue."

It can be used to take bits of chicken and turn them into chicken chunks or "nuggets." It can also take chunks of meat and glue them into a loaf of turkey breast, or a ham loaf. It also binds sausages and can even "glue" two skinny steaks into one big thick steak.

TG is found naturally in meat; it helps blood to clot and can be extracted from animal blood. Sadly, some people who know nothing about food OR cooking have said some bad things about TG. It is a natural product and nothing to be scared of.

Membrane. Found on the underside of ribs and if left on it can get hard or leathery. It should be removed. Take your fingers and loosen the white film on the underside of the ribs, rip it slowly and peel it off and discard it. If you don't remove it, the ribs will be tough and chewy.

Mutton. Lamb meat, actually meat from sheep older than one year so technically no longer called lamb.

Nappe. Pronounced nap. When liquid is thick enough to coat the back of a spoon and you run your finger across the spoon, it will leaves a trail for a few seconds. Sometimes called, "thick enough to coat the back of a spoon."

Parboiling. Boiling or lightly boiling food first before you cook it some other way. Raw veggies can be parboiled then set aside to finish cooking off later. It can be a time saver that doesn't harm the flavor. A friend of mine parboils ribs with an onion in the water. I don't like to do that, but she swears by it. Give it a try and make your own decision.

Planking. Before it was a fad where you lay down and mimic a board, planking was a method of bringing smoked flavor to meat in a closed oven. Yes. Who knew, right?

A wood plank, which is porous and aromatic, is soaked in water for several hours. The food is placed on top of the plank and the plank is placed over direct heat in a closed oven. The plank gets hot and heats the food. The water creates steam, the underneath of the plank burns creating smoke, and the food roasts and smokes at the same time.

If you are going to "plank" use only natural wood or wood bought at a lumber store that is clearly specifically labeled that it is to be used to COOK with.

DO NOT use construction woods for planking because they are often treated with poisonous preservatives.

Sautéing. To cook food in a small amount of fat over a high heat on a hot metal surface, like in a frying pan or skillet. Make sure the food is not too cold and the surface of the food is dry or the food will steam, not sauté. When cooking meat, or slices of veggies, make sure the pan is not crowded, food needs space. Sautéing onions and garlic makes their flavor less sharp and gives them a sweetness.

Savory. The opposite of sweet. Foods cooked as savory usually have spices that bring out main course flavors like salt, garlic and pepper. Although, sometimes, desserts can have a savory quality, like pepper.

Searing. To cook meat over a high heat for a short time to make it have a brown surface. Some believe that searing seals in the juices. My mom always seared her pot roast in a cast iron skillet before putting it in the big pot with the lid to slow cook for dinner.

Silverskin. A shiny, thin coating between the fat and the meat that will shrink and get tough when cooked. It should be removed before cooking. Use a sharp knife to lift the edges then you can usually peel it off with your fingers.

Simmering. To cook in a small amount of liquid where the bubbles are kept small, not allowed to boil but to cook slowly.

Umami. A very elusive taste. Other tastes are sweet, sour, bitter, and salty. Umami is best described as a deep and rich, warm, complex, and meaty flavor. Foods that are rich in umami are browned meats, soy sauce, sautéed mushrooms, cured meats, ripe tomatoes, and Parmigiano-Reggiano cheese.

Wet-Aged Beef. The process of aging beef in a vacuum sealed bag, usually for about 28 days. The process is different from dry aging because the meat is kept sealed and doesn't shrink. The flavor and texture of the meat is slightly changed, although not nearly as much as dry aging.

Wet-Cured Ham (also called City Ham). This is the most popular ham eaten in the United States. It is meat that is skinned and cured by soaking in a salt brine or injecting it with salt brine. Some wet-cured hams are cooked and labeled as "ready to eat." Some are sold uncooked as "cook before eating."

Always check and see if the ham you are buying is ready to eat or needs to be cooked. An hour before your guests are due to arrive is NOT a good time to realize the ham you bought needs to be thoroughly cooked before you serve it.

Whisked. Mixing a liquid or batter so thoroughly that there are no lumps and everything is completely dissolved. Whisking is easily and most often done with a balloon whisk. A balloon whisk looks like a balloon made of wires. Egg whites are usually whisked into a froth before folded in to a batter or whisked stiff into a meringue.

Thank you for reading,

"Food for Your Soul."

Even the simplest meal can be an act of ministry. As you cook the food and prepare the plates, ask God to lead, bless and empower all who eat.

(James 5:16b --The prayer of a righteous person is powerful and effective.)

You may also enjoy these devotion books by this author,

"Life Is Like Buffalo Breath" This is a devotional that uses endearing stories about pets and animals to illustrate Biblical Truth. Included are black and white photographs of animals. Also available as a Kindle book.

"**Whatcha Got? GOD Has Answers**" 42 devotions, a two part devotional. The first part deals with every day issues that Christians face, like anger, bitterness, and pain. The second part talks about things every Christian must have to live fully for Christ, like faithfulness, Bible study, fellowship and prayer. Also available as a Kindle book.

Also available is the book, "**Sick is An Attitude, Living WELL With Diabetes**." This is not a devotional; it is a book about living well for over 50 years as a Type I, insulin dependent Diabetic. It is written with humor while giving a lot of information on living well; available as both a Kindle e-book and in softcover.

Please watch for future devotion books by this author, annie keys.

Your Notes:

Made in the USA
Middletown, DE
19 June 2017